HEARTS WIDE OPEN

HEARTS WIDE OPEN

Leaving Religion, Finding Faith

Cedric Johnson, PhD

Hearts Wide Open: Leaving Religion, Finding Faith

Printed in the United States of America

Cover photograph from a painting by the author in 1992.

Luminare Press
442 Charnelton St.
Eugene, OR 97401
www.luminarepress.com

LCCN: 2023909072
ISBN: 979-8-88679-255-3

For Kris

Together, homeward bound

TABLE OF CONTENTS

FAITH TODAY

Prologue

The seminary building seems faintly familiar. Students drift between classrooms in a dreamlike state. Finally, someone stops and asks if I need help. I smile and say, "I'm okay," but I feel out of place.

Then a student glances at me and says, "Dr. Johnson? Didn't you teach here at one time?"

I give her a strained smile and nod. Do I know her? It's been years since I was last here. The start time for my new class is getting closer. I nervously check my watch every few seconds. I hate to be late. However, right now, I am going nowhere.

I notice a large room where the president and dean of the seminary and several elders from my evangelical church are seated at a conference table. They beckon me in. As they speak, I sit on the opposite side of the table, but I am spooked. What do these people want? The chair is uncomfortable and hurts my back.

"Why are you here today?" the president begins, grim-faced. "Did you not get our letter informing you that we no longer want you to teach?"

"That can't be true," I say, puzzled. "I have tenure. You can't terminate me without due process." My blood pressure rises, and I clench my fists under the table. I'm angry and confused. I lean forward. "What did I do to deserve this?"

"It is no use trying to defend yourself," he replies with an air of arrogance and spiritual authority. "You've gone wa-a-ay over the line. In fact, you've passed the point of no return! Students report that you seek to experience God directly in your soul, and you also challenge some of our orthodox teachings. For example, we were also told that you officiated a same-sex wedding. That is unacceptable." He pauses to catch his breath, and then, with gravitas, adds, "We find this tragic since a few years ago you sat right here with us as a peer."

Is this guy clueless? Doesn't he know that millions of people, especially young people, are deserting evangelical churches and other orthodox religions? And for good reason!

My heart pounds, and I fight the urge to jump to my feet and shout, "Many church exiles don't buy your dogma anymore, fool!" But I don't have the courage. Sweat pours down my face, and I can't catch my breath.

Just then, my eyes open wide. Above me, I see the beams on the ceiling. I glance around, disoriented. The bedding lies disheveled on the floor, and my t-shirt is sweaty. I get out of bed and stagger to the kitchen. As I steady myself against the back of a chair, I notice my ashen face in the mirror. I need a couple shots of caffeine.

"Damn," I mutter, "that was thirty years ago. When will this end?"

I stand alone in the dark, empty kitchen, and this seminary nightmare continues to haunt me like a horror movie playing over and over. Even after three decades, it still rocks my foundations, reminding me of the price I paid to leave the evangelical tribe.

But what price would I have paid if I had stayed?

Section One

LEAVING RELIGION

Chapter 1

TRIBAL BATTLES

During my decades as a card-carrying evangelical, a religious community I came to call the tribe, I was confident in my beliefs. Was the world created in six days? Sure. Did Jesus turn water into wine? Yes. Was he going to return to earth and beam me up into the clouds with other properly converted Christians? Absolutely. I was also instructed on how to behave as a Bible-believing Christian. I followed these prescriptions to the letter. Seldom in forty years did I buck the system.

My parents measured their devotion to Christianity by the number of times they attended church: twice on Sunday, once on Wednesday for the prayer meeting, and, for myself, Friday night for the youth group. Adherence to this rhythm was up there with obeying the Ten Commandments.

One Sunday morning at church, I was in the throes of one of my adolescent crushes. Before the 11 a.m. service started, I became engrossed in conversation with a young woman. Before we knew it, an hour or so had passed. We could hear the muffled sound of hymns and the pastor droning on and on. We were so wrapped up in each other that we forgot our duty: to sit silently on the hard pews and endure the service.

Afterward, I saw my mother bustling out of the church. Her face was red and riddled with anxiety as she confronted me.

"Your father is furious—why weren't you in church? What are you doing?"

My heart sank.

After we arrived home, my father sent me to my room to await my fate. He ordered me to take down my trousers and bend over the bed. I waited as I had done so many times as he went into the orchard and cut a long and flexible branch from a tree. It was an instrument of punishment intended to inflict maximum pain.

During the six splats on my buttocks, I refused to give him the satisfaction of my tears. I was seventeen. The spanking left me with dark bruises for at least two weeks.

An organization that majors in telling its members what to believe and how to behave often produces deep hurt. I discovered this much later when I worked as a clinical psychologist with evangelicals. One patient told me how the church had ordered him, a gay man, to convert to a heterosexual orientation or he would lose his leadership role in his church. The message? Deny your truth and conform to our beliefs about sexuality. I also saw the harm done to another patient whose husband physically abused her. When she asked her pastor for protection, he told her to submit to her controlling husband. There was even a cancer patient who was told he was dying because of a lack of faith.

I heard these horror stories in the early days of my psychology practice. While I was a pastor in South Africa, I had been unfamiliar with such legislation of behavior and belief. Hence, it took me a while to begin to understand that my patients were part of a religious and cultural system that was toxic and controlling. And though I searched for community aid for these folks, I didn't have a referral network of pastors who would support alternative and more authentic ways of behaving.

At the same time, I was beginning to challenge my own tribal beliefs. I stopped attending an evangelical church during this period and gravitated toward a more progressive faith orientation. What I once accepted as belief, for instance a literal view of the ascension of Jesus, I now challenged. My religious views moved from "I know for sure" to "I don't know, and that's okay." When the tribe mandated certain behaviors, I responded with a "Why?" Once, while visiting my parents, I clearly recall my mother pleading with me to attend church with the family twice each Sunday. I declined, and she ratcheted up the pressure (guilt?) by begging, "Please do it for me."

My response may seem cold-hearted to some, but I told her, "I don't make decisions that way."

The more I went against the grain of tribal doctrinal and behavioral expectations, the more I received pushback. Recently, an evangelical scholar read my memoir and commented, "I was hoping your intellectual and spiritual pilgrimage had landed you in a place where you still intellectually affirmed the historic doctrines of Christian orthodoxy." He also wished that I accepted "elements of the Christian contemplative tradition while embracing the guide rails of the historic Christian creeds." Perhaps to cheer me up, he added that his "assessment does not presume to render a judgment on either your relationship with God or your eternal destiny."

My struggle with tribal beliefs and mores began to expose the seeds of my heart-based longing to feel rather than just think about my religion. I started to search for the experience articulated by Jesus when he said, "Blessed are the pure in heart, for they shall see God" (Matt 5:8). At first, I could not put my finger on my heart longing to see or experience the Divine. In her book *Centering Prayer and Inner Awakening,* Cynthia Bourgeault identifies this inner or still small voice as "God's positioning system." She describes it as our "magnetic center" or an "organ of spiritual perception" that aligns us with God. Such direct inward spiritual experience eventually became a new direction for my faith.

Throughout this memoir, I explore my heart-based quest for what Rabbi Rachel Timoner, in an interview with Laura Esther Wolfson, described as "a strong belief that there is one God in the universe—one unifying presence that connects all life." My inner directed faith showed up in dreams, dance, visions, music, animals, nature, and meetings with ancestors. The more I sought direct connection with presence, the more I began to distance myself from a culture that focused on intellectual assent to a list of beliefs. Such cognitive rigidity or textbook belief often resulted in an immature and hateful religion. Amidst the swirl of dogma, my knife of doubt started to cut, one strand at a time, through a thick rope of tribal certitude.

My big break with aspects of past orthodoxy occurred on one quintessentially California sunny day when I attended a progressive Episcopal church in Pasadena. This Gothic-style revival church built in the 1920s drew me in. In the sanctuary, light refracted into rainbows through the stained-glass windows. The crowning event of that day, though, was the celebration of the Eucharist. It was here that I heard the following words: "Whoever you are and wherever you find yourself on this faith journey, you are welcome at our table."

Since childhood, in my South African evangelical background, the church restricted the Communion ceremony to the properly saved Christians who had experienced a conversion. Here, as repentant sinners, they gave their lives to Jesus. In this way, my Christianity became an exclusive gated community of, at times, judgmental tribal members. For example, if you believed that the Divine embraces everyone, you were labeled a Universalist. If you were gay, the tribe would accuse you of living in sin and suggest "conversion" therapy, exorcism, or, electric shock therapy. If you were divorced, it would be the occasion for raised eyebrows. But, of course, your chances of acceptance would improve if your spouse had left you (especially if they had committed adultery). And even today, God forbid you subscribe to a political position other than that of Christian nationalism, which demands you conform to their way of seeing or being in the world.

At All Saints, everyone was welcome at this sacred table. The inclusiveness was gobsmacking. Black and white, gay and straight, and even people like myself who were attempting to shake off the vestiges of evangelical beliefs were embraced.

I'm thankful every day that I backed away from the tribe. However, particles of my religious past persist. They cling to me like barnacles on a sunken ship. I still chip away at these intractable beliefs, as evidenced in my "church" dreams. In these night stories, narrated by my unconscious mind, my former peers criticize me for pursuing a nonconceptual faith. They remind me, "Your heart is deceitful; how can you trust it?" And they chasten me with, "Don't be led by your heart. Instead, lead your heart."

Today, I no longer cross the threshold of any house of religion. I never dreamed that I would find myself churchless. In the past, it gave me my identity, place of service, and connection with others. I often would refer to the church as my home. But as with any arc of life, some leave, and others stay. I chose to exit. In so doing, I died to my past just as I died to my physical connection with Africa. I know some who choose to stay in their tribal religion and hold their noses when they encounter certain beliefs. I have Roman Catholic friends who support a woman's right to choose but cringe when their priest rants against abortion. There are evangelicals who doubt a literal interpretation of specific biblical passages but remain devout church members. Each person has a reason for staying in the fold. Some remain for the sacred music. Others find comfort and meaning in rituals like the Eucharist. And then some value how their community meets the world's needs, like hunger and housing. As I ventured away from the church I found many such needs like community service fulfilled in a new network of exiles.

I did not leave the tribe in one sudden move. It was a gradual exodus. However, that's jumping the gun. I still had to wrestle with many more tribe-disrupting doubts and extract myself from a culture that held me in a vice-like grip from my earliest years.

Chapter 2

DOUBT, THE FLIP SIDE OF FAITH

I trampled on many toes when I refused to dance to the tune of tribal beliefs and mores. As I started to question particular evangelical dogma and practice, Bruce, the church bouncer, was not summoned to toss me out—but only because I left of my own volition. I was beginning to trust that doubt was an integral part of listening to the questions in my head and the promptings of my inner self.

As I explored my doubt, I confronted many of the tribe's head-based arguments by asking questions that put the noses of the defenders of church dogma out of joint.

What if we humans are flawed as well as created inherently good?

What if questions about divinity take us into a pure mystery that defies simple rational formulas?

What if the Scriptures are not the "norm" for every aspect of life?

Once, I expressed my curiosity about reincarnation to an evangelical pastor who abruptly declared, "I believe in the resurrection." I saw his mind snap shut like a mousetrap, and his clear message was, "Don't mess with my certainties!"

In another instance, at a church picnic, one of my seminary professors asked, "Do you believe in the devil?"

When I answered, "No, not a literal devil," I noticed a look of puzzlement on his face. It was almost as if he wanted confirmation for his growing doubt about this tenet of tribal belief. The dominoes of my lifelong religion were starting to fall, one at a time.

Amidst that whirl of mental conflict, I decided to join All Saints Church. A confirmation class was the rite of passage into this community. About thirty of us at various stages on the journey of faith assembled. Given my rigid evangelical background, I was struck by how diverse the group that assembled that day was in terms of age, religious experience, race, and their reasons for attending. Some were outright agnostics where any thought of the transcendent raised hackles. I felt like a reptile shedding the last vestiges of my evangelical skin. Throw a few atheists into the mix and one encounters a Dogma Doubt Fest.

All the class participants presented some version of show-and-tell with respect to their spiritual journeys. At first, I was reluctant to speak, but that reserve fizzled out as soon as the rector, the Reverend Dr. George Regas, began to talk. He was well known for raising hell and letting the chips fall where they may. When it was my turn to share, I confessed, "I can no longer recite the words in the creed." It felt radical and somewhat dangerous to admit this.

George's reply took my breath away: "You don't have to view those statements solely as literal truth to belong here. What you seek is not something handed to you by church authorities. It is something you intuit in your innermost being. Trust that and not humanly constructed beliefs."

How refreshing! Kicking the wheels of theology had been discouraged or forbidden in my tribal past.

A while later, a participant raised the question of the relationship of Christianity to other world religions. I squirmed a bit in my seat as I remembered how, in my early twenties, I had been an evangelical missionary in South America. Our mission was to convert others, even Roman Catholics, to our tribal club. As a wet-behind-the-ears seminarian, I even preached in a Pentecostal church in Rio de Janeiro, Brazil. I boldly performed my message in broken Spanish to a Portuguese-speaking congregation. I gauged that I was a success by their frequent "amens." I later realized these responses were about as helpful as likes on a blog. I could have intoned, "My black cat ate my hat," and they would have praised Jesus anyway.

That day in the confirmation class, though I was embarrassed by my former ways, I wanted to keep my old proselytizing tricks under wraps, so I asked a question: "I've never seen All Saints try to convert others to Christianity. Why not?"

Now red in the face, George sputtered, "It's the height of arrogance to think that we Christians have the only way to heaven. What happened to the millions who lived before Jesus? Could they not experience God?"

A chill ran down my spine. Finally, I'd found a place that viewed religion as a universal quest and did not exclude other faith traditions.

It so happened that I had invited a friend, a senior leader in the church I had pastored in South Africa from 1969–73, to join me at the class. He and his wife visited us in California, though we had not seen each other in over a decade. However, when we moved to the USA, we lost touch. So

I knew it was risky for me to bring him to the class. Yet a part of me wanted him to see my religious metamorphosis.

I observed him closely as the class progressed. He emitted occasional sighs and grunts when statements, often mine, questioned his cut-and-dried beliefs. On the way home from church, he squirmed in his seat until what had been bottled up popped out in a torrent of emotion. In a "Get thee behind me, Satan" moment, he shouted, "How can you accept what the rector tells you? You were so grounded in your beliefs. You've changed so much. What happened?"

Yes, what happened, indeed? How could I explain my shift from blind loyalty to a dogma inherited from childhood? How could my friend identify with someone who had made a midlife religious pivot away from the evangelical camp? For me, the inerrant Bible was out, and the symbolic interpretation of the Bible, Jewish style, became my new way of reading the Scriptures. "Only the born again gain access to heaven" was demolished, and the mantra "Everyone has a soul; that is the face we had before birth" became my mother's milk.

Predictably, my blatant discounting of our past beliefs disturbed my friend. He had no way of appreciating that my questioning process had become a prelude to a new dimension of faith. No wonder, then, that the discussion hit his panic buttons. Meanwhile, in the words of theologian Walter Brueggemann, I was beginning "to think the unthinkable, to imagine the unimaginable, and to utter the unutterable."

It was not just intellectual disagreement with the tribe around doctrines like the physical ascension of Jesus that stuck in my craw. I had a persistent internal blockage against feeling the world of the Divine. My role as the Bible answer person did not transform me. Doctrine seldom does. In fact, the more rigid my beliefs, the more my heart was tied up in knots. Here I needed actual role models of transformation of a heart set free to love.

In 1997, after a painful divorce, I met my current wife, Kris. Early in our relationship, I invited her to join me on Sunday at All Saints Pasadena. While the rituals and liturgy did not resonate with her, she listened closely, especially to the invitation to the Eucharist and the sermon. Several times during the service, she wiped tears from her eyes. Looking at her, I could not ever remember crying in church. "Why is she weeping?" I wondered. I looked around, trying to figure out what prompted the tears, and registered nothing.

Later in the car after the service, I asked what had triggered her feelings. She shook her head and said, "I don't know..."

Then, after a few more weeks of attending Sunday service and tearing up most of the time, she said, "I cry when I experience an alignment with something bigger than myself." Then she added, "I don't know what else to say. I know it doesn't sound rational."

Right there, I caught my first glimpse of a world I wanted to experience, one that arose from the heart.

Kris has a direct line to the world beyond our skin. I cannot count the number of times I have envied her non-conceptual and mystical way of connecting directly with the Source of love and the essence (or heart) of other people. I am reminded of the scene in the movie *When Harry Met Sally* where the Meg Ryan character has just simulated an orgasm to prove to the Billy Crystal character that she could fake one. When a server approaches an observer in the café, ready to take her order, the jealous customer comments, "I'll have what she's having."

How could I have what Kris has?

Chapter 3

A CHILD OF SPIRIT, NOT DOGMA

My attempt to know presence with my mind was an engrained, lifetime habit. Unfortunately, this "head first" history prevented me from having a more intimate relationship with God. The head eclipsed the heart.

My first introduction to knowing presence directly came while I was doing doctoral research on the religious conversion experience. My imperative was to stick to the facts, especially since it was a qualitative study. I did not suspect that an underlying capacity for spiritual (or, in this case, religious) conversion could include something other than our intellect. What I could not know then was that my transformation would not entail something to be reasoned through, but rather it would be experienced as another way of knowing. I soon discovered that knowing bone-dry facts alone seldom led to awe.

I was curious why people change and convert from one set of beliefs to another. I interviewed three professors and two fellow students about their transformation from nominal Christianity to a personal relationship with God. Until then, I had never met someone transformed by a direct experience until I interviewed my psychology professor, Lee Edward Travis, at his home in 1978. As the founding dean of the School of Psychology at Fuller Seminary in Pasadena, I was honored to be in his house and grateful that he had agreed to serve on my dissertation committee. Tape recorder in hand, and wearing my only pressed shirt, I was on a mission. My objective was to interview Lee about his experience with the world of the transcendent.

It was one of those crisp and eternally sunny Southern California days. Lee and Lysa's sprawling ranch-style home in the Bel Air neighborhood of West Los Angeles was situated in the lower part of the Santa Monica hills. I remember what I felt when I saw Lee on his home turf that day. He was the same warm, embracing man that dozens of other students like myself had routinely engaged with in class or on campus. It always blew me away that while other professors often gave perfunctory greetings as they walked by, Lee addressed each student by name and always took time to chat. He was one of the founders of speech-language pathology and was also vital in establishing one of the first programs in speech pathology in the U.S. at the University of Iowa. At the time of my interview with him, Lee was in his mid-eighties.

His powerful, direct experience with presence had come out of the blue fifteen years earlier. At that time, he had been a faculty member in the University of Southern California psychology department. He said he had attended very little to the world of the Spirit until then. As a result, he found himself solidly planted in a scientific, materialistic perspective. Lee described how his wife, Lysa, had invited him to Bel Air Presbyterian Church. The first Sunday they visited, the sanctuary was overflowing, so the service was broadcast outside to accommodate the large crowds. Lee described listening to Pastor Louis Evans, Jr. this way:

"I couldn't see him and had no idea what his appearance was. His voice was coming through, and the public address system could have been better. We sat outside. I was affected and carried away during his sermon, leaving the current situation and reality. It was as if I walked out and returned while the address went on. I didn't pay much attention to that. That Sunday ended, and I did nothing about that; we went home. Next Sunday, we went back."

The following Sunday, they arrived at church early to find a seat inside the sanctuary. Lee recalled:

"I could see [the pastor], which is when I had the intense experience. I had no visual experiences, and I didn't hear anything other than the preacher and the choir, so I had no visual or auditory experiences. It centered around mainly breathing, and I have great difficulty breathing, and the main thing that occurred was that the event carried me away.

"I never once thought that this came from within me. I always have felt, and still feel, that it was coming from the outside. I don't mean from the preacher or the music, but further than that, and because I don't couch this experience in ordinary Christian language, it loses some of its impact in the way I tell it. But, nevertheless, that's how it was.

"So mainly, I would be carried away, way out into the yonder. I was out there in the cosmos. I was part of everything in the world, the universe, and I was amazed at the largeness, and I was surprised at my privilege to be a part of this immense reality, and I would check to see what I was doing. There were two of me; there was this part of me that was way out there, looking over everything in the whole universe, seeing the end of time, seeing the beginning of time, seeing this, and seeing that I was a part of the entire thing and that I have always been here and that I would always be here. The other feeling is that an outside force occupied me. It was an experience that I could not interpret purely, and only psychologically. My mind was used. My body carried the feeling of being one."

In the end, Lee viewed this experience as an inexplicable direct encounter with what he called "heavenly reality." Pastor Louis Evans wrote of the significance of Lee's experience in 1961: "I see Lee as a son, not of dogma, but of the Spirit."

In late November 1997, at home in Altadena, I told Kris about Lee's mystical encounter. That was when she said she'd had similar experiences. We were sitting in front of a fire in my living room as Kris told her story. It was late afternoon, and the room was already starting to darken because it was autumn, making the fire seem brighter and more intense. I poured a glass of red wine for each of us. Kris said, "Last spring, I walked down the hall of the rehab facility [where Kris and I were working]. It was just after lunch. Most of the residents had retired to their rooms and were napping. The halls were hushed."

Working in the same facility, I knew this time well. The nurses and rehab team go off to the nurse's station to write their case notes or have lunch. The halls are empty. Kris continued. "I strolled, gazing into the rooms of each person I knew well, thinking about their life stories. One had been a commercial pilot. Another had owned a hat shop on Fifth Avenue in New York. Another loved to dance. As I thought of them, I felt affection for each one."

Listening to her at this moment, I recalled how Kris first impressed me with the way she worked with a patient with whom no one else in the facility could communicate. She instantly connected with the essence of the woman, quietly drawing her out to talk about her life and eventually answering Kris's questions. Kris also spent time with patients and their families after work. I remember thinking, "Why can't I be like that?" All I can think of when I'm in that facility is how fast I can finish the job, get out of there, and move on with the rest of my day.

I took a sip of wine and then turned toward her on the couch. She continued, "Suddenly, without warning, a force of energy struck me—a great power of Love. The energy force took control of my body. I was frozen in place. I don't know how long I remained that way, but as quickly as this love force had entered, it flowed out of me, leaving me physically shaken. My legs began to buckle, and I felt myself starting to fall. I quickly grabbed the metal railing along the wall and stood there, stunned. Then, feeling myself return to my senses, I was aware of the strength returning to my legs and that my face was wet with tears."

I suddenly felt a sense of déjà vu, remembering Lee's description decades before. Kris paused, looking out the window. I felt confused. I seldom cry and had never even heard of a love force. Yet, I could not wait for her to go on. She took a few moments before she said, "It was then that I felt embarrassed. I looked behind me to see if anyone was around. I then made my way to the outside door that led to the courtyard patio. I sat alone in a metal café chair at one of those small round tables for about five minutes while I regained my composure."

She reached for her wine. I wanted to ask her how long this had lasted and if she'd experienced this before, but then she said, "It probably lasted a couple of minutes, but it felt like time had stopped."

She seemed lost in her thoughts for a few seconds, and I did not know what to do. I had all sorts of questions that I sensed I should not ask. Then she added, "That was when I remembered I'd had this experience one other time. Eight years prior, an energy force of love entered me while riding a horse on a carousel in Central Park in New York City. I was thinking of my deceased grandfather, who used to take me to a carousel in Chicago and watch me go round and round as a very young child. The carousel started to rotate, and the horse I was on slowly rose and fell, establishing its rhythm. I imagined my grandpa standing off to the side on the grass, smiling and waving at me each time I came into view. It was peaceful, like the feeling of slowly letting go just before we fall asleep. I remembered how it was to be with my grandpa, feeling our mutual joy and the warmth of his love."

At that moment she sat up, leaned toward me, and, putting down the glass, looked up at me intently. "Then suddenly, this incredible force of energy in the form of pure love hit me, so powerful it overwhelmed me. Because I was straddling the horse, I wasn't aware of whether my legs weakened. That experience lasted longer than the one I told you about earlier. It only subsided once the ride was almost over. It also left me in tears. Finally, the carousel stopped, and I remember shaking as I dismounted the horse and stepped off the carousel.

"Two friends were waiting for me, sitting on a bench nearby. Seeing my disturbed, tear-stained face, they stood quickly and anxiously asked what was wrong. I remember

I couldn't stop crying. We all sat down on the bench. I tried to explain, saying, 'I just experienced this tremendous force of love, this massive bolt of energy.' I paused, wondering. 'It was as if my dead grandfather just visited me.' They both laughed, and one said, 'Don't say, "as if he visited me." He DID visit you, yeah, he visited you alright!'"

Kris seemed very pensive as she added, "Later, even though I'm agnostic, I wondered if thinking about him had somehow caused his spirit to break through. Over the following months, I had a recurring thought: I never knew he loved me so much."

Her eyes welled up with tears.

I stared at her, mystified. How does that happen? I pray often. She doesn't seem to pray at all. She continued, "It's important to say that these mystical experiences are divorced from any other experience I've had. The Love I felt in both those moments was not an emotion that wells up from within. Instead, this force of Love entered my body and seemed to take over my entire being. In those moments, I felt I'd surrendered control to this force that now inhabited my body. Also, it came as a total surprise—instantaneous and powerful, entering at full strength, unlike human love, which expands more like a balloon. This Love felt vast as well as powerful. Human love feels more like something that can fit into the size of a drinking glass, while this Love is like an endless ocean with no horizon and no boundaries. I'm amazed that love can be like this when I think of it. It's not human. It's something else."

I felt despondent. "I often pray," I said, "but that has never happened to me."

"Maybe you don't need it," Kris replied. "You've been on a spiritual path all your life. I don't subscribe to beliefs, but

I feel now that there is something more than we can know with our analytical minds."

I still wanted the direct knowledge of the Divine that I saw in Lee and Kris. I began to search for that knowledge with something more than, but not excluding, my mind. When I was an evangelical, I knew a lot about God. Those were my head-generated beliefs. However, although I knew about God, I did not *know* God experientially. Eventually, that direct knowing is how I came to define faith.

Arriving at my internal destination or heart has been a convoluted process. First, I had to deconstruct many of my old tribal beliefs and behaviors. The chief agent for my paradigm shift was my encounter with a truth-teller, the disrupter that I married.

KNOW ~~ABOUT~~ GOD

Chapter 4

LIVING WITH A TRUTH-TELLER

It was 7 p.m. on a Sunday. The strains of Mozart's clarinet Concerto in A major wafted through the air. I was about to start my weekly radio show, *The Next Step,* on an evangelical Christian station in Southern California. It was a call-in program where listeners would consult me, a psychologist, about their problems in life.

That evening, Kris was painting the living room walls. She was also listening to my radio program, as she did every week. Suddenly her attention was caught by an advertisement that aired just before my show. As she listened, the words she heard caused her to lay down her paintbrush in shock. The announcement advised listeners who had businesses not to hire gay people.

When I returned home later that evening, Kris confronted me. "I heard an announcement on your show discriminating against gays. That is outrageous."

As Kris and I discussed the issue, I explained, "I told the engineer not to play that on my show and move it to a later airing."

Kris shook her head, rejecting my rationalization. "I

don't think you want to be on a radio station with ads intended to discriminate against others because of their sexual orientation."

Kris spoke the truth to me. Still, I continued to resist her input. Why?

First, I had so much skin in the game with this radio show. My program had been airing for nearly fifteen years. The Arbitron Ratings indicated a growing audience. Moreover, I gained satisfaction from being a radio talk show host.

Her confrontation rattled me. I couldn't shake it off. Eventually, I got her point and realized that I needed to take a principled stand. Still, I waited to act on my conviction. Instead, I futzed for a few more weeks, looking for a compromise. Throughout, Kris did not back down from her challenge. She reiterated, "The ads may not be on your show, but they are still broadcast on that station."

Eventually, I yielded. I broadcast my last show and resigned in what today I consider a less-than-courageous way. I did not object to the station's management about their ads. Instead, I slunk off the scene after a clumsy farewell. The reasons I gave the listeners for my leaving did not address the point; instead, I said I was starting a new phase in life as a corporate consultant. The only redeeming factor about quitting the show this way was that I made a definitive break from my religious tribe.

At the time, I did not fully realize the gift of Kris's truth-telling. Eventually, I stepped back to look at the things that mattered, like taking a stand to affirm and protect a person's sexual identity as his/her human right. In the process, I also tore off my blinders, enabling me to see, for the first time, the true nature of my tribal culture.

Finally, I learned that silence is complicity.

This experience made me think of other occasions when I had remained silent in the face of injustice. My earliest memory of being too afraid to speak up was during a conversation with my father when he left Zambia for a new life in South Africa.

"Can you comprehend what our family cook said when we were about to drive off to South Africa?" my father asked. "He reminded me that he has worked for our family for nearly two decades. He then had the gall to ask me for a pension."

I felt disgusted in the pit of my stomach and ashamed that my dad did not have the decency to give our long-term employee a retirement stipend. My father had the money. He had recently sold his three houses in Zambia. However, since avoidance was my typical response in the face of difficult conversations, I remained silent.

This pattern of overlooking injustice took years to break. In the early 1970s, I pastored an all-white Baptist church in Natal, South Africa. On Sunday afternoons, a Black group used our building where a visiting pastor led the service in Zulu. Being Baptists, we had a pool in the sanctuary that we used for total immersion baptisms of adults. The Black congregation needed to fill the pool for their baptism ceremony on Sunday. On this particular evening, our white group also had a baptism service. A group of white leaders approached me with a request: "We cannot use the water from the afternoon service tonight. We need to drain and refill the pool."

This angered me. "Absolutely not!" I said, thinking, "Do they believe that the water would be contaminated because Blacks were using it for baptism?"

After I adamantly stood my ground, to my surprise, not one of my church leaders opposed my decision.

If I had to do it over today, I would have gone even further and challenged the leaders' premise about the "dirty" water. But, unfortunately, it took years before I recognized injustice and protested publicly.

Kris is honest and direct with me. She forces me to look in the mirror. With her intelligent kindness, empathy, and refusal to suffer fools gladly (including myself), she sees to the core of an issue or person right away. She also sees things long before I do.

People have chipped around the edges of my self-deception and denial before, but never in the way Kris does. Before her, my coping strategy was to push such situations out of my mind. I can rationalize that I am not an activist by nature or tradition. The likely explanation is I turn away from painful situations rather than sailing right into the storm. I am learning that tumultuous waves don't necessarily overturn a boat. I need to stay at the wheel and steer the ship according to principle.

Kris was not the only one to propel me out of the darkness of denial into the light of awareness. The other big event was my move to the United States of America.

Chapter 5

MY FRENCH ANCESTOR

Who was Louis Fourie from the 1600s, who sailed the ocean blue to South Africa? And what's the story of the ship *Walloon* that bore my nineteen-year-old ancestor to South Africa?

Often, when I reflect on who I am and wonder how my ancestral roots shaped me, I find myself magnetically drawn back through time to Louis Fourie. He was my mother's namesake several generations ago, my many-times-over great-grandfather. He was the young man who boarded a Dutch East India Company (DEIC) merchant ship in 1688 and sailed from Holland to South Africa to start a new life. Like myself, a sense of adventure drove him, and an inner divine calling prompted his leap of faith.

What made this young man tick?

I can only imagine.

He probably stood on the dock at Texel, an island north of Amsterdam, with about forty other Huguenot émigrés. He sensed he was about to embark on one of the most dangerous voyages in the known world. For months he had frequented local taverns and listened to tall and not-so-tall tales from old salts that had made that treacherous journey to the Cape of Good Hope. Finally, he heard how the DEIC was looking for a few good men to settle in South Africa and farm the land to supply these ships. This adventure was not without its risks. It was not unusual for a tiny boat like *Walloon* (160 feet long and thirty-eight feet wide, and weighing 892 tons) to sink as it plowed through the fierce and harrowing storms of the Atlantic Ocean. Possibly, he would have to fight pirates alongside the soldiers aboard the *Walloon*. He would need to find the will and guts to survive scurvy and unending seasickness (with its resultant dehydration) and very little drinking water.

Hardship always shadowed him. He was driven out of Dauphine, France, for being a Huguenot. His family had been under severe persecution by the Roman Catholic hierarchy. Louis fled his country after the revocation of the Edict of Nantes in 1685. That edict upheld the right of freedom of religion for Protestants in France. It permitted them to hold public worship in many parts of the kingdom, though not in Paris. However, when Louis XIV formally revoked the edict, French Protestants lost all religious liberty. Like many Huguenots of his time, Louis found his way to the land of religious freedom in Amsterdam. At first, he experienced Holland as a friendly haven for his Calvinistic Protestantism, but cultural displacement became a fact of life.

Louis was a Frenchman in Amsterdam.

At the crack of dawn, after hearing of the DEIC job offer, he joined the line of applicants outside their headquarters. The nervous chatter, mainly in French, was about any snippet of news from back in Dauphine. Then there were rumors that the DEIC was also sending young orphan girls to the Cape of Good Hope as marriage prospects for these girl-hungry boys.

A wizened, weather-beaten old seaman named Oupa (Dutch for "grandfather") beckoned the boys forward one at a time for the interview. First, he gave him the lowdown on the job. "You get a free ride to South Africa. If you make it there alive, you get one hundred acres to grow supplies for our ships. Also, if you return before five years, the deal is off. So sign here," he said, pointing to a document with his grubby finger.

Not my idea of a kindly grandfather, Louis may have thought. However, before Louis could trip over more of his rising doubts, Oupa pointed to the other side of the room. A glazed-eyed group of Huguenots was slowly gathering before what looked like a Dutch Reformed *predikant* (pastor).

"It's the swearing in," mumbled the old man.

After Louis signed the agreement with the DEIC, the pastor administered the oath. That day, some applicants declined to sign up on the pretext that they were averse to the sea and long voyage. They changed their minds and decided to settle in Germany instead. The others set sail for Africa from Texel on July 27, 1688.

We can only imagine Louis's relief and excitement when he finally sighted the Cape of Good Hope six months later, on January 27, 1689. According to tradition, the first person that saw the famed flat-top Table Mountain was given a silver coin by the captain of his ship. Upon landing, the ship's captain, Karel Goske, delivered a letter and the Huguenots to the governor of the Cape Colony, Jan Van Riebeeck. It contained instructions from the DEIC for him to give the new settlers a warm welcome and basic supplies for their agricultural venture.

History is silent about his first year in the Cape. Like his move to Amsterdam, the first community Louis sought out was the Dutch Reformed Church in Cape Town. Within a year of landing, Louis moved to his new property. Here his hundred acres of scrub-covered land took many backbreaking months to clear before he could even develop it into what eventually became the Slangrivier vineyards.

Louis eventually assimilated into the South African culture. His Calvinist roots and strong work ethic made his transition to the new culture easier. But, unfortunately, some persecution and cultural domination continued as he was forced to speak Dutch and not French by the governing authorities in the Cape. That Dutch evolved into Afrikaans, which became the language of my mother, Elma Fourie.

A belief in the Divine sustained Louis's optimism and rugged determination, which echoed his Calvinist religion. He had heard the sermon dozens of times as the *predikant* told his white-skinned congregants, "The Lord has a special plan for us. You are children of the covenant, chosen for a special mission in South Africa." The minister quoted from memory the ancient Hebrew text: "And I will establish my covenant between me and thee and thy seed after thee in their generations for an everlasting covenant, to be a God unto thee, and to thy seed after thee" (Gen 17:7, King James Version)."

These starry-eyed Huguenots appropriated the ancient promise to Israel. Then, finally, Louis heard the antecedents of future racial policies in the apartheid regime that kept the "natives" in their place as servants. The pastor very likely added another biblical story. He viewed Blacks as the descendants of Noah's son Ham, described in the Bible as dark-skinned. He would have gone on to recount that Noah planted a vineyard and produced wine after the great flood. One day, in a drunken stupor, he fell asleep naked in his tent. His son happened on the scene and saw his naked father. When Noah awoke and realized what Ham had seen, he cursed Ham's son Canaan in a rage. The Scriptures record, "Cursed be Canaan! The lowest of enslaved people will he be to his brothers" (Gen 9:25, King James Version)."

Over the years, many members of Louis's church used this biblical passage to justify the slavery of the Black people brought from other parts of Africa to the Cape. In her book *Caste: The Origins of Our Discontents*, Isabel Wilkerson writes, "The story of Ham's discovery of Noah's nakedness would pass down through the millennia. . .the biblical passage would be quoted to condemn and to justify the kidnap and enslavement of millions of human beings and the violence against them."

Louis's sense of white supremacy became my cultural heritage. I never thought about it and felt entitled to get first dibs on many privileges reserved for whites.

Louis's human-made, God-endorsed tradition became the roots of the future apartheid racist political system. Whites viewed themselves as having been chosen to rule the black-skinned people who, according to the Dutch interpretation of the Bible, were cursed by God. The Bible even states, "Now therefore ye are cursed, and there shall none of you be freed from being bondmen and hewers of wood and drawers of water for the house of my God" (Jos 9:23, KJV).

There is nothing like divine permission to encourage folks to exploit another ethnic group. In the USA, President Polk, in the nineteenth century, reframed racism and expansionism in terms of the doctrine of Manifest Destiny. Unfortunately, these children of the covenant in the USA adopted a similar destiny to dominate others.

Only after I migrated to the USA did I become aware of the roots of my racism. As I observed the boycott of everything from sporting and entertainment events to the export of U.S. goods to South Africa, I became aware of the heinous nature of racism. However, South Africa was not the only racist society. As I conversed with a Black friend in the USA, he said, "Every day I leave home, I am aware that I'm Black. You have no idea how afraid we are to be pulled over by a cop, even for minor traffic violations. We feel that our life is on the line."

Another part of what Louis believed to be a Divine Plan was when he met and married Suzanne Cordier in 1695. She became the mother of his ten children. After her death, he married Anne Jordaan in 1716 and had eleven children with her, who became my ancestral line in South Africa.

As an aside, I discovered recently through a genetic test that I have 2 percent Black blood coursing through my veins. I was delighted when I revealed this fact to some of my relatives. I am not as white as my South African family once thought. What's the genesis of that story? I love my tiny piece of solidarity with a people once relegated to the margins of life.

My family trip from South Africa to the USA in the early 1970s was a breeze compared to Louis's. We had eighteen hours of flying time and the minor inconvenience of being stranded at Heathrow during the labor strike. I lost my wallet (which contained my passport and credit cards) at a phone booth (returned by the airport staff), and our biggest hassle was managing two squirmy toddlers. However, the reality was we were still migrants and descendants of migrants.

We all hope for reliable crystal balls. We plan, guess, and wish, but in the end, our departures put us where we are today, living with a series of new beginnings. Like Louis, I experienced a fresh start spurred on by the ideal of "One nation under God, indivisible, with liberty and justice for all." However, as I bumped into racism in the USA, I began to see that those lofty words in the Pledge of Allegiance were aspirational. Unfortunately, what U.S. citizens often miss is that those words were seldom on the lips of white South Africans during my years in the country.

There is no hint of liberty and justice for all amongst the majority of the ruling class, the white Afrikaner population. Instead, it celebrates the history of invading ancestors, Louis's relatives, who followed their God-given calling and conquered and suppressed the Black nations.

I better understand my sense of white male entitlement as I reflect on the history of such attitudes in my family and country of origin. History does not have to be a person's destiny. We don't have to be reactive toward and fearful of each other. Instead, we need open-heartedness and safe places to break bread together and tell our stories. We also require our equivalent of the Truth and Reconciliation Commission initiated by the new and independent South Africa leaders to deal with past crimes against our fellow citizens.

Quite apart from the cultural conditioning that left me with a legacy of white privilege, I also had other emotional disabilities that churned around in my psyche and kept the door of my heart jammed shut.

Chapter 6

DUCK AND DIVE

One of the saddest things I saw in a bird park in Asia a couple of decades ago was an eagle with its wing feathers clipped. The zookeepers also chained the bird to an iron stake in the ground, destroying its potential to soar in the heavens.

The eagle experience may have affected me so profoundly because I recognized that I, too, was destined to soar with heart-inspired love. However, like that magnificent bird, my emotions were constricted. My recurring theme was, "Don't get too emotional with others." I felt restricted in my capacity to fully enter their world. Yes, as a psychologist, I learned to empathize with my patients. I needed some of that capacity to be a helpful therapist. However, in my personal life, I felt as though I never came fully into my emotional self. I realized this recently when I told Kris she was the first person I had ever loved. I identify with the words of James Baldwin, "Not everything that is faced can be changed, but nothing can be changed until it is faced."

I had to face an event from early childhood that was part of a plausible explanation for why, over the years, I shut down emotionally. However, one swallow does not make for summer. That childhood experience was not the only cause for my emotional constipation. Other factors include how I was socially conditioned as a male not to express feelings (except for anger), my British roots that gave me a stiff-upper-lip approach to hard times, and my mid-life crises that helped build my defensive wall.

I'm five years old. It's been a rough day at the grandparents' house. It is 1947, and I live in central Africa. Memories of World War II, when some of our soldiers were part of the Allied forces in North Africa and Europe, are fading fast. However, my grandfather still calls England home since it was his father's birthplace, even though he has lived in Northern Rhodesia for decades.

He wears the typical colonist "uniform"—khaki shorts and long woolen stockings—and his knobby-kneed legs stick out from his oversized shorts like match sticks from a barrel. He has no advanced formal education. Yet, despite that, he is a self-taught builder and house designer. His speech, often peppered with obscenities, mingles with blue cigarette smoke as he strides quickly past half-amused Black workers at the building site. Today I trudge alongside him with my skinny legs and baggy shorts—a veritable chip off the old block.

The altercation starts when I return home and repeat a few juicy swear words within Grandma's earshot. She freaks out, but what's the big deal? I mimic him. I'm a fast learner of all things profane. As a performer personality, always conscious of my audience, I soon notice that my cursing has a maximum dramatic impact, especially on Grandma. She's a strong-willed enforcer of "proper" language and social etiquette. My curse words bring the long arm of her law slamming down on me. Today she says to me through pursed lips, "Use that word again, and I will wash out your mouth with soap."

half-mile track event at age eighteen. That accomplishment set me up for the regional track meet two weeks later. Yet, even now, when I recall it, I shudder at the memory.

I line up for the start of the 880-yard run. Adrenaline courses through my veins. At the starter's gun, I surge ahead of the rest of the competition like some wild horse galloping across the prairie. At the halfway mark, way ahead of everyone with an unprecedented time of fifty-six seconds, I am about to smash the national high school record in less than two minutes. I only have 100 yards to go. Suddenly, I fall to the ground in pain with a severe leg cramp. In agonizingly slow motion, I stagger to my feet and stumble toward the finish line. The other runners catch up to me. My teammate pushes me over the finish line, which leads to my disqualification. I collapse again. My chest heaves as I lay on the side of the track, gasping for breath. I am vaguely aware of other athletes anxiously hovering over me.

"Are you OK?"

The soundtrack drowning my heaving breathing is not inspiring, like something out of *Chariots of Fire*. Instead, it is a depressing dirge played over and over in my head—for years to come. The inner voice repeatedly asks, "What if?" and laments, "If only!" If only I had warmed up for the race properly. If only I had paced myself better on the first lap. If only I did not have a go-for-the-gold mentality in all that I do.

At the time of the race, I did not know what drove me toward the finish line other than the desire to win and win big. In those days, I never linked my performance to my personal value, but it became my modus operandi in later years. I sometimes call it my ego swagger. So many life lessons caused me to crash and burn in the decades that followed. In the end, I seem to have earned a PhD in failure.

Each incident pricked the bubble of my ego illusions. The shelf life of my "I am my doctorate in psychology," "I am the books that I publish," "I am my global consulting experience," or "I am my white male entitlement" all had an expiration date. Yet, decades later, I still agonized over the what-ifs: What if I had not fallen that day and become the national champion? What if my whole life direction would have changed if I had won that day?

In recent years, I've realized I am not the sum of my likes or dislikes or failures and successes. Neither is anyone else. The problem with performance-based living is that it's a drug-like ego fix. I squirreled away a stash of achievements in case detoxing from my ego became too painful. Today my ego fixes come in all shapes and sizes. How many likes did I get on my blog? What was the size of my audience? Did people like what I did on that project? Now I realize these ruminations are typical in a stage personality like mine. They distract me from the world of my true self—the self that I cannot break. That self is impervious to hurt and remains whole and intact in this life and beyond. That home needs no improvement program. All masters of the spirit declare that our chief purpose in life is to discover and live out the soul's essence and not seek the fool's gold of the ego.

My performance is starting to fade with time. At long last, it's beginning to dawn on me that I'm too old for this crap. Besides, most people are too self-absorbed to care about what I do. Hence, I bother less and less about impressing others as I slowly discover inner contentment and security. My pointless and repetitive mental gymnastics are nothing but an illusion or a bad dream.

I began a sputtering meditation practice about a decade ago. Here, I had the opportunity to discover, in silence, a new part of myself. Somewhere in my being is an indwelling and eternal consciousness beyond my brain. Many names are given to this force like God, Yahweh, Soul, Krishna, and Presence. The force is not produced by our brain. It's like saying that the Stradivarius violin does not produce the music; instead, the musician does.

At first, those moments of consciousness came somewhat infrequently and in whispers. I observed it during a coaching session when an inner voice prompted me to shut up and listen without judgment. It tells me to focus on serving others rather than proving I'm a good coach. In other instances, flash insights about the client bubble up with a highly plausible explanation. My gut speaks long before my lips move.

Some time ago, I was listening to a highly talented young woman who doubted her natural abilities. Most saw her stellar writing talent. She published in peer-reviewed journals. By all measures of writing success, she had made it. Yet, in her thinking, she saw herself as an imposter. To add insult to injury, she criticized herself for being too ego-driven. She lamented that she was too focused on the positive reviews and devastated by the occasional critical remarks. Her belly-button-gazing led to the paralysis of analysis. Here is where our discussion went:

CJ: Do you see your writing ability as a divinely given talent?
Writer: In some ways, I do. Something comes to me out of the blue when I'm in the flow. It seems as if some outside source is channeling through me.
CJ: Have you ever heard of the saying from ancient Hindu writings, "Do your duty to God without your

eyes on the fruit of your action?"
Writer: Yes, I have.
CJ: "Just do it" is easier said than done. What do you think about learning to silence your inner critic, not looking at reviews, and getting back into the flow? In other words, you have an inner voice. Use it.
Writer: Let me think on that point.

As we parted, I gave her a quote from Neale Donald Walsch to ponder: "Yearning for a new way will not produce it. And ending the old way is just the starting line. You cannot hold onto the old while declaring that you want something new. There is only one way to bring in the new. You must make room for it."

My friend did not have a sudden "A-ha" moment. However, the seed we sowed in our discussion that day germinated over the next several years. As she focused on her craft with a daily writing ritual and got out of her own way, her inner critic became less pronounced, and her creative juices began to flow again. Where did that inspiration come from? I cannot explain how it happens when I see evidence of something within us. However, I know that in those moments of insight, I see proof of our true identity, the eternal presence within. It's not something I have to add to my life through achievement. That's who I am.

Chapter 8

MY BATTLE WITH THE BIBLE

Most former evangelicals like myself have a love/hate relationship with the Bible. Yet, one part of me finds it a source of inspiration. I'm encouraged when the ancient Hebrew writer of the Psalms finds hope in troubling times. However, my inner skeptic has a "How can that be?" response to stories like a man walking on water. The last time I tried it, I almost drowned.

For four decades, I lived in a bubble of a dogma-centered evangelical group that described themselves as the "People of the Book." They believe every word inscribed in Scripture and pronounce it as a normative guide for all time. So when the apostle Paul tells women, "And if they desire to learn anything, let them ask their own husbands at home; for it is improper for a woman to speak in church (1 Cor 14:25)," is he covering up for some male insecurity?

The Bible is the story of personal or national encounters with the transcendent world. But before the Scriptures became the written word, it existed as an oral tradition. Obviously, none of us were in the initial audience. Instead, the authors addressed the readers of their day through the lens of their own cultural perspective. For example, during the exodus from Egypt to the promised land, the formerly enslaved people encountered local resistance. They claimed God told them to stamp out the enemy. Is that written record a mandate for genocide today?

My battle with the Bible began in 1983 when I wrote the book *The Psychology of Biblical Interpretation*. In it, I point out that human thought and emotions play tricks on our supposedly rational thoughts when we read the Bible. It's always challenging when we impose our interpretative bias on any situation. My training as a psychologist showed me how our minds distort what we view, from witnessing an accident to interpreting a text. When evangelicals claim, "We don't interpret the Bible, we just read what it says," they seldom take into account reader bias. That's one explanation for why there are so many different ways of affirming these "truths" amongst the various branches of Christianity.

My next move drove the tribe crazy: I questioned the absolute authority of the writers of the Scriptures. They, too, were subject to internal and cultural bias similar to that of the reader. These ancient Jewish authors spoke through myth (something universally true). Turning water into wine is more than getting a great bottle of Cabernet from the backyard faucet. The miracle is about the transformative nature of an authentic divine/human encounter.

The whole penchant for literal interpretation came onto the scene in the first centuries after Gentiles became a part of the church. The title of John Shelby Spong's book is *Biblical Literalism: A Gentile Heresy*. That literalism persists today in orthodox church circles.

Even in my most ardent evangelical days, I found it a stretch to believe that while divinity was revealed in Jesus

2,000 years ago, he was God's first dance with us humans. I taught world religious traditions at the university level in the late 1990s, and I was struck by how each major world religion subscribed to the tenet "love your neighbor as yourself." Also, in considering ancient Eastern religions that predate Christianity by thousands of years, many of their sacred texts have similar themes to the Bible, like creation stories, the flood, and miracle stories.

Quite a few students from the evangelical traditions were in my class. They were at first horrified that I, as a supposed Christian, was teaching the universality of truth. But then, they asked, "How can you call yourself a Christian if you do not see Christ and the Scriptures as the only way to God and a manual for how we live our lives?"

When I started to comment on the possibility of a heart-based knowing of the Divine, their hackles were raised even more. They reminded me that the human heart is wicked and cannot be trusted. I then presented the challenge that millions of folks over hundreds of thousands of years outside of the Judeo-Christian tradition had direct experiences with the world beyond and within. Where are those folks today? In hell?

The Bible or any sacred Scriptures are but one way to encounter the transcendent world. Consider gut knowing (intuition) and direct awareness or consciousness of presence in each of us. Such knowing through an inner operating system has various names like the image of God, the soul self, or the eternal consciousness. It's an internal homing device that comes from and leads to the Eternal One.

Trusting the revelation of presence at the center of our being has become the holy grail of my search for truth. But I cannot achieve this goal by myself. I need Divine aid in that quest. My inner operating system had to coax me toward an experience of presence. This fact alone is a blow to my ego, which prides itself on figuring out the mysteries of life. Humility is, therefore, a necessary precursor to knowing presence directly.

I discovered a faith of my own along a road lined with tribal protestors. Some placards read, “Get out of here, you heretic,” or “How could you betray the foundations of your faith?” or “We found it, you lost it.” Such protests were a prelude to my being shown the exit door.

Chapter 9

NECESSARY LOSSES

The world for which you have been so carefully prepared is being taken away from you by the grace of God.

—Walter Brueggemann

As happens in the granddaddy of TV reality shows, *Survivor*, the tribe voted me off their island. I bucked the system, paid the price, and earned a place in exile.

Nearly three decades ago, my first wife Ann and I were on vacation in Hawaii when we received a call from a hospital in Chicago. The nurse informed us that our youngest son Bevan, in his late teens, had been admitted to their psychiatric unit. He was attending a youth conference representing his church. Late one night, the conference organizers found him barefoot in the snow. They became highly alarmed and had him admitted for evaluation at the hospital.

We cut short our Hawaii vacation and returned to California. On the return flight, I ruminated on my conversation with a therapist at the Chicago hospital. A thousand questions swarmed in my mind. Was this run-of-the-mill adolescent confusion? Had we missed the precursors to that episode? Unfortunately, as trained mental health professionals, we both overlooked the evidence of a significant mental disorder. Instead, we assumed he was going through a "phase" when his college studies took a nosedive before this trip.

The admitting therapist at the Chicago hospital started probing to evaluate what we, as parents, had done to contribute to his current mental breakdown. He had to be kidding. While I admit that some of my parenting skills needed improvement, like my being too hands-off and disengaged, I took umbrage at the insinuation that we had somehow caused this major mental breakdown. Three days later, Bevan returned to California. Three hospitalizations and years later, we settled on a diagnosis of schizophrenia, a physiologically based disease that causes significant cognitive and behavioral distortions.

During the years of his illness, I felt as though I was driving in a fog. I missed the hazards on the road ahead in my marriage of twenty-three years. I became highly self-absorbed. I escaped from my distress by numbing out at work. On a typical morning, I saw several psychiatric patients at a hospital. Then, I drove through heavy traffic to my Santa Monica office for over an hour in the afternoon. Here I would consult with four or five more clients. Finally, I would retire late for the night after another lengthy commute. I was exhausted, slept poorly, started gaining weight, and fell into a mild depression.

Meanwhile, our once-mild-mannered, kindly son Bevan was now sailing through stormy emotional seas. His confusion added to my distress, helplessness, and guilt. In response, I retreated into the cave of my misery.

At the same time, Ann and I became increasingly distant. All we seemed to talk about were ways to manage our son's disease. We lived with pain, pain, and more pain. Eventually, we began to associate each other with the trials of this crisis. But, unfortunately, I was so preoccupied with my pain that I could not fully appreciate her struggle.

Several months later, I reached out for help from a psychotherapist. She, too, had a son who had schizophrenia. I found the sessions extremely helpful. Her explanations, like "It's his disease speaking, not him," normalized his occasional vitriol towards us, his parents.

Ann caught me by surprise when she told me she had consulted my therapist and asked to join us in an upcoming psychotherapy session. At the time, I was totally in the dark about why she wanted to attend the session. I knew we were going through tough times, so I assumed she was seeking some resolution for our marital difficulties. What followed hit me like a bolt of lightning. Ann looked me straight in the eyes and said, "I want a divorce."

When I blurted out, "Why?" no explanation came. Instead, after a few minutes, Ann stood up and left the session. I sat there silently for what seemed like an eternity. It felt as if all my life's dominoes fell at that moment.

For the next several weeks, I ranted and raged at the therapist as I tossed and turned before I fell asleep. I yelled at the skies, asking, "What did I do?" as I frantically rode my bike for hours. I hated how my therapist had conspired with Ann and betrayed our therapeutic relationship by allowing Ann to use that session to inform me of the divorce. I felt ambushed and even thought of suing the therapist for her breach of confidentiality. But, out of my old habit of avoiding conflict, I shut down the anger after a few weeks and never returned to therapy.

I never made complete sense of the reason for the divorce. Ann had an emotional affair with an aide at the hospital where she worked. She talked endlessly about him and his romances with other staff members. I was also surprised they invited me to join them at a comedy club in Hollywood. I was so dense that I did not realize she had become deeply attached to him. What I did recognize, however, was that our marriage was in a deep freeze.

I needed clarification as to what was going on. A few weeks earlier, we saw the Barbara Streisand movie The *Prince of Tides*. Here, the main character, a psychiatrist, falls in love and has an affair with her male patient. I mostly forgot about the movie. However, I did mull over the ethics of a therapist having a romantic relationship with a patient. The fact that Ann was in love with a coworker reminded me of the Streisand character in the movie. So when she told me, "You will have to fight for me," it was a warning shot across my bow, saying, "You need to do something about our marriage." Unfortunately, I needed more information. I regret that her warning came too late. She already had plans to leave the marriage. This separation was not what I wanted for our life together. I never imagined in a thousand years that I would become a divorced man.

The fallout from that fateful therapy session nearly three decades ago went far beyond my hurt and confused feelings. I love the title of Gloria Steinem's book, *The Truth Shall Set You Free. But First, It Will Piss You Off.*

My ensuing divorce pissed off a lot of folks in the tribe. In their estimation, much blame for the marital breakup fell on my shoulders. How could a leader with a psychology-based talk show on a Christian radio station, a frequent speaker in evangelical churches, the director of a psychological clinic that primarily served the religious community, and a former ordained minister be terminating his marriage?

It did not win me points with the tribe that Ann wanted out of the marriage. I was their point person—hence, I was to blame. I kept asking myself how I could have taken her for granted and focused more on my work than on my marriage. I now accept my part in the separation. Many marital problems occur when one or both members in a relationship become emotionally detached. That was, in part, our story. However, there were many culprits in this marriage breakup. Maybe she was feeling trapped by our circumstances. Perhaps she wanted to move to Hawaii, where she eventually migrated and married on a surfboard. Such questions are now purely academic. Anyway, I was left to muddle on with my life as it unraveled over the next several months.

At that time, I was teaching a couple of psychology courses at a local university. My hurt spilled into the classroom. The students were alarmed at how I blurted out my divorce story in class after class. They marched en masse to the dean and complained. I was summoned to the dean's office, and he terminated me from my teaching assignment.

Soon other doors began to close for me professionally. I applied to teach a psychology course at a seminary, but they turned me down. I put two and two together when I heard they had terminated other divorced professors.

I was tough on myself for that marital breakup. The criticism of the tribe rubbed salt into my wounds. Some of my friends, including a couple that taught marriage counseling at a local evangelical seminary, mused, "We were so shocked at you and Ann getting divorced. You seemed such a solid couple. If it happened to you, we were afraid it could happen to us."

The reaction from the local churches we served as a clinic was even more dramatic. The referrals dried up. And so did my speaking engagements. Suddenly, my friends either took sides with my soon-to-be-ex-wife or dropped off the map. All this rejection nudged me away from the tribe.

The fallout from that failed marriage lasted for about a decade and bled into my romantic relationships. I bounced from one doomed dating situation to another, my clinic fell apart, and my sense of purpose in life became blurred. I found myself enjoying my work as a psychologist less and less. As a result, I began to dabble unsuccessfully with a career in public speaking.

My financial world lay in tatters. The debt from my son's hospitalizations started to pile up. At one point, I had no food in my refrigerator, no money in the bank or pocket, and I seriously contemplated living out of my car.

Amidst these painful episodes, I glimpsed some of the flaws in the tribe and myself more clearly. Despite ubiquitous divorce rates in the church, judgment was heaped on couples that broke up. Even Ann's reassurance that I was a good person as she walked out the door did not mollify my situation. I had the scarlet "D" inscribed on my reputation. Hence, it was no surprise I reverted to the ancient belief that I was unlovable. This alarming message stuck in my psyche like an embedded fishhook despite the fierce loyalty of some friends who stood by me. Beyond this small group, I would give the tribe a solid "F" for how it responded to me amidst my floundering confusion. They jumped from acceptance to virulent rejection in a flash. "We love you if..." hurts under any set of circumstances. Conditions of worth can sever strong friendships, communities, and family ties. As one friend told me, "If you raise hell, be prepared to burn."

Little did I guess that the furnace of adversity would heat up even more over the next several months.

Chapter 10

SALT IN THE WOUND: THE CHARADE

I wanted to write something other than this section. That's because my ego had the need to look good and ignore any hint of a major flaw. I don't know how many times I've been asked by tribe members, "And how many times have you been married?" That judgment was salt in my already open wound.

Most of my professional life was in West Los Angeles. I'd heard of All Saints Church Beverly Hills from friends. It was known as a supportive community, and the rector, Carol Anderson, was famed for her inspiring sermons. Still swimming in grief, I drifted there after Ann left me. While the Pasadena All Saints Church had drawn me toward my social responsibility and was my exit from the exclusivity of the tribe, the Beverly Hills All Saints Church held me in the arms of a more contemplative expression of faith. Pasadena was about Jesus, the prophetic revolutionary who spoke truth to power; Beverly Hills embraced me through the Wounded Healer. I would sit and weep silently during the Sunday morning worship service. Yet, strangely, I also felt filled with hope and encouragement. Desperately off course spiritually, I needed something to ground me. I also found a source of distraction.

I noticed this tall, striking blond, as did a crowd of mainly male admirers who surrounded her after church services. I forget what the class we attended was about, but I vividly remember her praying aloud as the priest encouraged us to do. It was brief and straightforward. I was curious why she addressed Divinity in a childlike way, saying, "Papa."

At that time, her parents were front and center in her thoughts. She had recently returned from their fiftieth wedding anniversary celebration in a small university town in the Midwest. During those few days with the family, she had decided it was time to return to church and get her spiritual life back on track. In some ways, she wanted to replicate their lives. They were upper-middle-class folks with solid community ties. Zoe longed for a more stable, community-centered lifestyle, preferably one in which she could retire from her work as a costume designer in the movie industry.

Zoe made me look good. She served as my instructor in Impression Management 101, especially in how she upgraded how I dressed. Upon reflection, I recognize that my dating her and our eventual marriage was my way of trying to normalize my position in the community. It was an image-based attempt to heal the wounds of my recent divorce. Ultimately, it was my little effort to construct a success story to bolster my sagging self-esteem.

We were the beatific couple on the wedding cake as we soon dove into the ministries of All Saints Beverly Hills. I became a eucharistic minister who assisted in the weekly Sacrament. In addition, we both volunteered to serve meals to the homeless in West Los Angeles. I was back in the saddle again. Or so I thought.

At midnight on New Year's Eve, while dancing at the Ritz Carlton Hotel in Pasadena, I yelled out my marriage proposal on the dance floor to the strains of "Somewhere Over the Rainbow" playing in the background. She responded in her pronounced Southern drawl, "You bet ya, by golly."

Our home soon became the setting for gatherings of church folks and an assortment of her Hollywood friends. She even invited a former fiancé and his wife for dinner. I felt it was her saying, "See? I made it." We hosted social events, from swim parties to staging my fiftieth birthday party. The Cedric Improvement Program was now in full swing as I was propelled back into the center of a church community.

A few months later, at a premarriage church retreat, the priest warned us we were rushing into marriage and should consider waiting a while. Looking back, I see he was 100 percent correct. Nevertheless, I stubbornly wanted to normalize my life again and figured marriage would do it for me.

A week before the marriage ceremony, I assisted our priests in the Eucharist. Part of my South African family was in the congregation that day. As I hurried around officiously, carrying the chalice of wine from one congregant to another, my robe curled around my legs. That led to the mother of all trips. The wine spilled all over the altar area, stained my shirt, and left a red Rorschach-like image on the smooth altar floor. A somewhat bemused Rector Carol and another assistant helped mop up the mess. My face was now the color of the wine.

A week later, my ego-self had an impression management ego-boost at a well-choreographed marriage ceremony fit for any Hollywood production. To add to the drama, not one but three priests officiated. Did that give it the *Good Housekeeping* stamp of approval or what? I was genuinely charmed by the whole event. During the recessional, I jumped in the air on our outward glide and clicked my heels like some tawdry Fred Astaire imitation.

The energy lift from that nuptial production carried me through the following year. However, years later, I realized something did not fit my marriage charade. My decisions had more to do with ego inflation than planting my feet on solid ground. The seeds of destruction were there from the very beginning. The undertow of debt from my divorce and my son's frequent hospitalizations kept dragging me down. And then, my private practice dwindled. I threw myself into a new professional venture, a series of workshops on topics like "Live Your Dream" and "Success in Marriage." Today I recognize a certain irony in the title of the marriage workshop. Yet again, I allowed myself to be blindsided by a failing marriage. I also had blinders on concerning my professional aspirations with respect to motivational seminars. Veteran professionals advised it would take years before these ventures became profitable, and that I should keep my day job as a psychotherapist.

My heart was no longer in being a therapist. I purposely turned down new clients and closed one of my two offices in West Los Angeles. At the same time, I leveraged my radio program to promote my seminar business. The public response was reasonably good, with twenty to thirty people attending each event. Zoe pitched in, helped me administer the workshops, and sold my audiotapes and books. During the same period, she launched her career as an accomplished artist.

Another issue began to eat away at me: Zoe's attitude toward Bevan's schizophrenia. Granted, she saw him at some of his sickest moments. But she sometimes seemed to believe he was merely acting out. She found it very difficult when I received phone calls from Ann on how to deal with Bevan's crisis. It reached the point where I eventually had to sneak off to a nearby pay phone and call Ann from there.

Six months into our marriage, my hospital job ended.

The harder I worked on this new life, the more it seemed to tank. All the while, I refused to look at the reality of my financial situation. Instead, I kidded myself, thinking one more series of seminars would keep me from drowning. Finally, Zoe saw the writing on the wall, which scared the bejesus out of her. She held on for at least another year before my financial stress overwhelmed her. And then, unbeknownst to me, she began planning to exit the marriage. All her alarm bells sounded when we were forced into a bank-mandated short sale of the house. She had wanted to leave full-time employment in the movie industry. Now she had to take on part-time seamstress work that did not bring in enough to bail us out. Gone were the plans for a secure life like that of her parents. Slowly the relationship began to sour, and we became distant. Zoe confided in her parents, friends, neighbors, and even the priest that she planned to leave me. Everyone knew about the pending divorce. I slowly realized my massive mistake in getting married so quickly. However, the well of my reputation started to be poisoned.

We never built a love foundation to endure the storms. Filled with guilt and remorse, I sought out the priest who married us and asked for the rite of absolution. He stunned me by saying, "Cedric, I've known people like you all my life. Quite frankly, you're a bullshitter. "

A bullshitter? Me?

Those words stuck in my craw for years. However, I find solace in the words of Bryan Stevenson: "Each of us is more than the worst thing we've ever done." But back then, I was riddled with guilt and remorse and took to heart the priest's honest assessment.

Although I agree there was a certain bravado in how I tried to promote my new business, my self-promotion efforts were sincere, if misplaced. I was afraid, and all my bold talk about career plans was like whistling in the dark as I passed the graveyard of a failing life.

That half-assed absolution from the priest was another nudge for me to leave the church. It had once been a haven of refuge and a venue to live out ways to serve the community. Now my flailing efforts became a source of judgment. Many of the folks I knew avoided me and started to give me the eye. My paranoia heard them saying, "How could you get divorced from a wonderful person like Zoe?" and "What did you do wrong?"

Looking back at that marriage, I realize I did what I told patients never to do—jump into a new romance and avoid the resolution of past hurt. As a result, I give myself two strikes with the double divorce track record.

After the dissolution of yet another marriage, it took several months for my life to turn upward. I'm profoundly grateful for the gift of two teachers that came my way in the following years: Kris and our adopted dog Oaxaca. Each taught me about what it means to be in a loving relationship. And both provided me with a solid foundation for my career in leadership consulting with global organizations. Sometimes things happen that break our hearts and throw us into the pit of despair. Fortunately, other forces at work in my life gave meaning to this turbulent period captured by a passage from the Hebrew Scriptures: "As for you, you meant evil against me, but God meant it for good" (Gen 50:20).

That turnaround is another memoir in and of itself.

Section Two

THE TEACHERS APPEAR

The old Buddhist saying, "When the student is ready, the teacher appears," applies to my journey toward the world of spirit. The timely appearance of these instructors came after two divorces, my son's schizophrenia, severe financial hardship, and while I was slowly extricating myself from the tribe. I willingly walked out the back door, where exile beckoned to me as a better choice than a life of compromise and conformity.

One teacher was my future wife. Another showed up in an adopted dog.

Chapter 11

SLIDING DOORS: HOW WE MET

Twenty-five years ago, I interviewed for a job in a most unlikely place, a skilled nursing facility. That was the last place on Earth I once would have seen myself working as a psychologist since I knew very little about treating geriatric patients. Also, at that point, I was moderately depressed. Amidst this slump, I was approached by a consulting group to interview for a job in their network of geriatric and rehabilitation clinics. On the day of my interview, I dragged myself from one facility to another. I tried to project as much bravado as possible. However, my heart was not invested in securing a position.

Toward the end of the day, my future boss, Ron, took me to what he considered one of their top-notch centers. Although we had scheduled an appointment, the director did not show up. There would be a two-hour wait before we could meet with her. Ron saw my eyes droop with disappointment and said, "How about we try one more place a few miles from here?" Grudgingly I agreed.

We schlepped across town for what I thought would be a somewhat routine interview. Midway through the process,

Ron said, "There's someone I want you to meet. She's a speech therapist and has a background in psychology. She could be a terrific source of referrals for you."

He ushered me toward a nondescript office where this person was on the phone. After a brief wait, he introduced us. "Cedric, I'd like you to meet Kris, the speech therapist. And Kris, this is Cedric, a psychologist interviewing for a job here."

Kris seemed preoccupied with some patient-related issues. That was a good sign. She probably would not want to spend too much time talking, and I could retire for the day and do something I enjoyed, like take a long bike ride.

Kris emerged through the office doorway, backlit by fluorescent lights. She appeared like some ghostly apparition from another world. She glanced at me and seemed distracted in the middle of our introduction. Then, I noticed a sudden shift in her demeanor. I only found out much later the significance of her distraction. She explained, "After introducing us, Ron announced that this gentleman would be starting as the new psychologist at our facility. At that moment, I was startled by an internal voice resonating in the middle of my head. The voice, firm and clear, was redirecting me. 'It said, pay attention to this.' As I refocused my attention on you, what struck me again was your emanating presence, something I've rarely experienced with anyone. It felt powerful without being intimidating."

I knew nothing about Kris's internal message until some weeks later when she said, "As I came to know your values and character more, I had a déjà vu moment. Had someone told me about you weeks before I met you?" Musing on that, she continued, "Eight years before meeting you, I'd consulted a highly recommended, gifted intuitive, Mark, who I hoped could help me understand some intuitions I was having that were disturbing me. After that, I didn't see Mark again for many years. I had another session with Mark though a few months before meeting you.

"I remembered that Mark mentioned in that session that I would meet someone. At the time I was in a long-distance, tortured relationship. Introducing another man into my life my life was crazy. It would've added another layer of complication to my already disturbed life. Consequently, I barely registered this information. We recorded our sessions, so I pulled the tape and listened to it again.

"In May," Mark told her, "God will guide you—don't panic when I say this—God is bringing a new male into your life. This unknown male will be a friend, probably an associate, and you will agree that this is a genuine emotional, spiritual, and soul connection. This new male connection in your life is by design.

"Another reason it will happen is it will raise your awareness of how another man can relate to and connect to you. It will cause you to become more aware of your needs as a woman, and as a human being, and, most importantly, what you have a right to receive. You will also learn where you have overcompensated [for another] at the expense of your own needs.

"You have been growing and maturing these past years, so you will not shut down or deny this new perspective even though it will make you uncomfortable.

"The new relationship is about a friendship and the perspective of another man who gets you. This [new] relationship will result in higher emotional self-esteem. You were born brilliant, but your humanness is starting to emerge alongside your brilliance. Something inside of you is demanding that your life grows into more wholeness. You have already put the contract out there, and there's no turning back, which is why I know a new person will come into your life to give you a new perspective. For now, you need to make time to practice the art of stillness and the art of doing nothing.

"It will be profound what you will receive in clarity. You are accustomed to doing the work to understand, but if you give yourself time to be, you will receive clarity. You don't have to go to it. It will come to you. You've always survived and succeeded using your brain; now, you are transferring from your head to your heart."

"After listening to the tape," Kris said, "I suddenly remembered the 'voice' that had come to me when you and I met: 'Pay attention to this.' I immediately connected the dots. I cannot help thinking that there was some destiny in our meeting."

I took the job. Afterward, I ensured I had many "chance" encounters with Kris. I would wander into the nursing station where she was writing case notes and start a conversation while I wrote up notes from my patient sessions. Sometimes I would walk into the rehab room where she was having coffee, drape my leg casually over one of the desks, and slide back to sit on the desk's top. By nature, I have a confessional style of sharing information, so I opened up on a wide range of personal topics with Kris.

For example, I told her I had a radio talk show about psychological issues called *The Next Step*. I must admit I was trying to impress her. Her academic background in psychology and communication and her love for radio piqued her interest in this topic. During all these conversations, I wanted to get to know Kris. She was the person I wanted to be around more and more. She was bright and highly educated and had done seminal research in her field of study.

One day, I told Kris I felt unequipped for the job. "I've never worked with older people with cognitive deficits, and, quite frankly, I find it pretty dispiriting."

She paused. "Hmm," she said, "maybe you're taking your job too seriously. You know, yesterday, one of my patients thought the lunchroom was a dance hall!"

I looked at her, puzzled. "How so?"

"Well, I was in the lunchroom when lunch had ended. All the residents in the room—women—had fallen asleep in their wheelchairs. I was very quiet. I looked over toward the door and saw my patient rolling up to the doorway in his wheelchair. He looked intently around the room. Then he cupped his hands around his mouth, like this, and yelled, 'Do any of you ladies need a ride home from the dance?'

"Every day is filled with surprises like this," she said, "you can't but help fall in love with the patients."

I came to know Kris as kind and sensitive, with a tremendous capacity to see the true essence of even the most difficult people. That brings me to Ariel. Ariel was in her mid-eighties and had recently suffered a stroke, though her speech and language had remained intact. The other therapists had been unable to obtain her personal information for the intake. They warned Kris that Ariel was uncooperative and difficult to engage. Before I knew Kris well, I stood in the hallway and watched her treat Ariel. Kris was remarkably attuned to her. She spoke in a soft, low voice and waited patiently for Ariel when she did not respond immediately. She went off script, asking Ariel about her life—where she lived, her work, and her family. They were in a rhythm that Ariel, not Kris, controlled. Kris showed genuine interest;

she was very kind. Watching her treat Ariel drew me even more to Kris.

Later, when Kris left the nurses' station, I caught up with her and said, "I was standing in the hallway, watching you treat Ariel. You were so amazing with her, the way you drew her out."

She looked up at me, perplexed. She studied my face. Then she said, "Look, I'm no Mother Teresa!"

"Oh, no, no," I said hurriedly. "I'm not into saints; I like people with an edge."

"Good!" Kris cheerfully responded.

It was inevitable that we would eventually treat the same patient. Kris described it this way. "Gloria was a long-term resident at the facility. She had cerebral palsy and had been confined to a wheelchair most of her life. She was intelligent and engaging, and I enjoyed chatting with her. Her radio was always on, tuned in to Classical KUSC. On several occasions, Gloria told me she suffered from chronic depression. Knowing she could use some support, I referred her to Cedric. Cedric had been treating her for a while when one afternoon Gloria waved, beckoning me into her room. 'I think my psychologist, you know, Cedric, I think he likes you,' she said.

"I said, 'Yeah, I know him. He's charming.'

"Gloria responded, 'He likes you. Every time you pass by, his head turns to the hallway.'

"I laughed. 'Gloria, many people walk down this hallway.'

"'No, he turns to you, not to anyone else.'

"I didn't know how to respond. Was one of the few sentient patients in the facility now playing matchmaker with rehab team members? I felt the heat rising in my face.

"'No, no, Gloria,' I said, shaking my head. 'Uh-uh.'

"Then I stood up and abruptly walked out, hoping she wouldn't repeat this. I was a private person, but I took note of her observation. Maybe his interest in me was more than a passing chat at the nurse's station."

The connection I experienced with Kris was in stark contrast to life back home. There, my relationship with my second wife was falling apart. The marriage vow "for richer or for poorer" had long evaporated. In fact, during a counseling session with our rector, Carol Anderson, at the Beverly Hills church near the final days of the relationship, Carol said, "Zoe cannot keep her wedding vows. She is terrified by your financial situation. That is why she has decided to leave. And quite frankly, Cedric, you need to fix your finances. I hear they're a mess."

My job interview was a desperate stopgap move. The same was true for Kris. She needed to make money fast for dental work that cost a fortune. The job was the most lucrative opportunity available in her profession then. Quickly my professional conversations with Kris bled into other areas of common interest. She had lived and worked in England, and I once was a British citizen. One founder of her speech pathology discipline, Dr. Lee Edward Travis, was one of my professors and someone I admired. This fact alone intrigued her.

The first day we went to lunch was November 5th, 1997, Guy Fawkes Day, a memorable day in British history. Having lived in England for over four years, that date was well known to her. We were so open and comfortable together as if we'd always known each other. When we returned to work, she said, "This is the best time I've had with anyone in months.

The following week we went out for lunch again. After

the meal that day, I suggested we go to a movie. I knew she had scheduled herself to work that afternoon, so I was delighted when she agreed to play hooky. Again, I took note of her willingness to break the rules. It revealed an edge I admired.

Soon we were spending every day together, and our bond grew. One evening we found ourselves at a small Armenian restaurant in my neighborhood in Pasadena. We were the only patrons there, and as had become typical, the conversation became intimate and spirited. We sat across from each other, and most of the time we leaned forward with our faces about two feet apart. There was lots of laughter and continual eye contact. Halfway through the dinner, I became conscious that the owner and his friend were standing behind the counter staring at us. As we were about to leave the owner strolled to our table with the check and said, awkwardly: "My friend and I were watching you two. We made a bet that you asked her to marry you. Did you?"

Kris and I looked at each other, unsure what to say. She turned to him grinning.

"We've only known each other for three weeks!"

The owner smiled and gave us a knowing look. As we were getting into the car, I squeezed Kris's arm. "Can you imagine how they thought I proposed to you? That's something. What do you think?"

She smiled back at me warmly but did not reply. The owner lost his bet that evening.

I floundered emotionally, and before Christmas 1997, one of the last vestiges of stability dissolved. My family home for over a decade in Altadena sold on a bank short sale. By then, Kris had visited the house and noticed no food in the fridge. She got the message quickly that I was navigating choppy waters. At one point, I decided it was time to give away my furniture to the Salvation Army, but they passed on the offer. They considered the furniture below their standards because it was too old and damaged. The next option was a dumpster. It was tough to give up the house that had been the family base for over a decade, the one stable thing in my life. I sold the house at a loss, which did not sit well with me. I pleaded with the real estate agent to help me at least stay in the place until Christmas. She declined my request. Where could I go? I needed money to stay in a hotel.

Then came one of those moments of serendipity while she lived temporarily with her sister while she saved her pay for dental work.

However, she had sensed it was time to move on and search for her own place. So one day, when she was at work, I offered to go house hunting in South Pasadena—an area she had had her eye on for some time. While still in England and considering returning to the USA, Kris had dreamed of living in a 1920s cottage with hardwood floors and a large fireplace. That day I saw a "For Rent" sign outside a property where five such cottages were situated. It was built in the 1920s, as a community for seamstresses, and was now occupied by renters.

Unfortunately, there was a long waiting list for that particular cottage. Kris was determined to get it. She met with the landlady and told her this was precisely the cottage she'd dreamed of for years. Kris broke down in tears. That sealed the deal. That became was our first home together, where my close friend Harry Evans, married us (unofficially) in a private ceremony before the fireplace. That was November 24th, 1998.

And to think, we never even dated.

We knew early on we were destined to be together. Looking back at our meeting, I marvel at how I was given the gift of a heart-based relationship. Kris, an agnostic, was the exact opposite of the tribe women I had been dating. Most of them had a clear set of religious beliefs. By contrast, Kris is a natural-born skeptic. She questions authority and is unconventional. In this way, Kris greased the wheels of my growing doubts about my tribal dogma. She also had very progressive political views. For someone like myself from a racist and sexist community, I was being dragged (quite willingly) into a world of greater inclusiveness and equality.

Our fateful meeting reminds me of the movie *Sliding Doors*. Here the protagonist Helen, (played by Gwyneth Paltrow), takes us through one of those "What if?/Timing is everything" moments. The movie presents two possible scenarios. One is where Helen, running a bit late that day, misses the subway by a split second (hence the sliding doors). In the other version, she makes it through the train's doors. The film plays out the results of both scenarios. Two entirely different outcomes for her life ensue.

My missed appointment with the nursing director led to a change of plans and an interview in Kris's facility. Thinking of the incredible life I have had with Kris for more than twenty-five years, I shudder to think what my life would have been like if the first interview had materialized and I had ended up working there. What brought us together? Was it divine intervention? It certainly wasn't because of my good judgment about romantic relationships!

Chapter 12

MY DOG, MY TEACHER

"I dedicate this book to my beloved fifteen-year-old Black Lab, Venus, whom I had to release to God while beginning to write this book. Without any apology, lightweight theology, or fear of heresy, Venus was also Christ for me."

—FR. RICHARD ROHR, *THE UNIVERSAL CHRIST*

Falling in love with a dog can be a formula for heartbreak. But, of course, that's true for the death of any beloved animal in our lives. Yet, as Fr. Rohr suggests in the dedication to his book, that animal and cherished friend remains a presence to us. My first significant experience with loss came in a pup we named Oaxaca. She lived with us briefly, and we were devastated when she died.

I stumbled down the long staircase, carrying the lifeless body of our beloved Oaxaca to Dr. Luciano Carrasco's car. A few minutes earlier, Kris and I had held her as this loving Mexican veterinarian injected a muscle relaxant that caused her to melt into our arms. He looked up with compassion in his eyes as if to ask, "Are you ready?" We nodded, and slowly and deliberately, he administered the lethal dose. Kris placed her ear to Oaxaca's chest to listen to her last heartbeats. A few seconds later, she died.

Luciano kindly offered to have her cremated. However, after he delivered her body to the crematorium, he decided the ashes container was unsuitable for a dog we loved. And so, in a great act of kindness, he constructed a special box for her ashes.

How did this once-emaciated, abandoned dog worm her way through the creaky door of my heart? How did she, a simple street dog from Mexico, teach me life lessons that hundreds of hours of theology and therapy did not accomplish?

As I rewind the clock by seventeen months, Kris and I find ourselves at Rebecca Raab's forty-acre ranch outside the village of San Pablo Etla, near Oaxaca City, Mexico. Situated on rolling hills, a casual walker could scratch the ground with a walking stick and uncover pottery shards from the sixteen ancient indigenous groups.

Ostensibly, the farm produces agave, a cactus-like plant that yields mescal. However, it is far more than an agricultural business. In the early 2000s, ranch co-owner Rebecca Raab started the Friends of Megan Animal Rescue nonprofit. The organization is named after her beloved German shepherd Megan, whom she brought with her from Washington State. Megan's death was a catalyst for the founding of the animal rescue mission. Today it is a veritable Noah's ark, housing stray donkeys, horses, dogs, cats, and birds. All have the opportunity to find a forever home through adoption. As Rebecca developed a reputation for her mercy mission, locals started bringing (sometimes dumping on her doorstep) stray animals.

We had been living in San Miguel de Allende, Mexico for about one year when the travel itch took us to Oaxaca, the land of the Zapotec and Mixtec peoples whose forbears date back to 11,000 BCE. Before we knew it, an emaciated, abandoned dog, looking like a concentration camp survivor, appeared out of the blue and wormed her way into our lives. One ranch activity was the daily sweep for stray animals in the surrounding villages. One day, Kris joined Rebecca on one such rescue mission. They spotted a lone golden retriever mix in town. It immediately became apparent the dog was on the point of starvation, as could be seen by her protruding ribs. She was skittish and dodged human contact—no doubt because the locals habitually threw stones at her and shooed her away from their houses and stores. The young people laughed derisively when rare scraps of food were thrown to packs of dogs. Nobody could touch this ghostlike white dog that disappeared as mysteriously as she had appeared. Kris and Rebecca named her White Dog.

We were in our car, crawling along a pot-holed Oaxaca road on our way back to the ranch from a visit to another art-filled village when the phone rang. Rebecca told Kris, "We've captured White Dog and taken her to the animal hospital to be spayed, fed, and bathed."

Kris started crying but said, "I'm so happy and relieved that she is going to be OK."

Knowing quite well by now that when Kris is crying, some truth is gurgling up, on a hunch I haltingly asked, "Would you like to adopt White Dog?"

Without batting an eyelid and with even more tears, she replied, "Yes, and I know what I will name her. Oaxaca."

"Let's find out from the vet if she has medical issues, and then we will," I cautiously replied.

Later that day, Rebecca brought White Dog to the ranch. First, we saw and felt her protruding rib cage as we petted and stroked her matted fur. Then, Kris took Oaxaca's face in her hands and slowly opened her mouth. What she saw was appalling. The dog's teeth were half the expected size, split in places, and dirty brown.

"How did this happen?" Kris asked, thinking of the suffering the dog must have endured.

"Probably when she chewed rocks trying to extract morsels of sustenance," Rebecca answered.

We had never had a dog during our relationship, never mind an adopted stray in such poor physical condition. On the first night in our rented house at the ranch, Oaxaca slept on a makeshift bed of folded blankets. Rebecca gave us some dog food that Oaxaca wolfed down before anxiously looking around for more. She was also hyper-vigilant with our cats. The dog growled whenever they came near her food bowl. After a while, we noticed her enlarged nipples and concluded she had recently given birth to a litter of puppies. Although we grew more tender toward her, she remained highly suspicious of us for weeks.

We were curious why Oaxaca would never look directly at us. Her face was always downcast as if to reflect some unknown and primal sadness. It took months for the bond of affection to develop. On our daily walks, when off-leash, she would never let us out of sight but constantly turned and looked back. Within several weeks, she was no longer the dog with her tail between her legs. Instead, she was the happiest dog in the village. Locals repeatedly made remarks about her furiously wagging tail.

True to her retriever genes, she was passionate about fetching her ball. This routine started within a few days of her arrival. I would endlessly toss that orange rubber ball, and she would always wait for more until my arm got tired. She even chased the ball a few days before she died.

Oaxaca became an inseparable part of our lives for the next seventeen months. First, Luciano told us she was two years old. Later we discovered she was eight. We needed to believe our dog was younger to sustain the wish that Oaxaca would be with us for many more years. We joked that she was our Velcro dog. We never wanted to let her out of our sight. When we left her in our room, she patiently waited at the door for us.

Oaxaca traveled thousands of miles with us on many road trips. The places changed, but our bond with her was constant. Whether we were in San Miguel de Allende, Mexico or Vallejo, California, a typical day in the life of Oaxaca looked like this: At the crack of dawn, she would approach our sleeping selves and go to each side of the bed and greet us with her cold and wet nose. Then came the ball routine. She chased her ball on the beaches of Northern California to the shores of Lake Michigan, from the Aztec ruins in Chiapas, Mexico to the trails of Point Reyes National Seashore in California. We took her to almost every beach in Northern California. We also stopped countless times for the ball-throwing routine at obscure road stops.

It was only a short time before we adopted terms of endearment for her like Oaxaca-Bear-Bear or Best-Dog-in-the-Whole-Wide-World. She would howl with delight when we put her on a leash for a walk.

In January 2012, while we were in Northern California, she stopped eating and drinking. She could no longer jump into the car, so we hoisted her onto the back seat. Next, she developed tumors on the joints of her legs. Then a growth the size of a softball appeared on the side of her neck. It grew alarmingly more prominent by the week. Eventually, this oozing wound hinted at more serious problems. She would yelp with pain when we touched her neck. Finally, a vet examined her and intimated that she was dying. She became increasingly fragile. Kris slept with her on the floor and fed her water a drop at a time. She pleaded with her not to die. Despite all the signs of imminent death, Oaxaca hung in for another few months. These efforts on our part gave us enough time to take her from California back to the place where she had probably been born in Oaxaca.

We kept glancing at the back seat to see if she was still alive. We traveled across the USA and down into central Mexico. We even ventured to the southern border of Mexico to the state of Chiapas to see the Mayan ruins. At the end of that trip, Oaxaca was again listless, and her strength was lagging by the day. We covered her wound with a colorful bandana that made her look dapper, but we knew she was near death.

When we arrived at our friend's house, the rescue team, including Rebecca and Luciano, sat in a circle around her. She lay listless in our midst, dispassionately eyeing the proceedings, oblivious of what was about to happen. Her white fur glistened, and occasionally she groaned quietly. Kris and I held her in our arms and whispered words of love and consolation. Tears streamed down our faces as Luciano drew the syringe with the lethal formula. Then, as Oaxaca drew her last breath, we cried, groaned in anguish, told her how much we loved her, and finally whispered goodbye.

I had to leave on a consulting trip to the USA the next day. As I left the house, our host told Kris, "I don't feel comfortable with him leaving. He looks so much older. His face is gray."

I felt like a zombie for the two-hour flight to the USA. I then dragged myself through the Houston airport to catch my next flight. When I came to an escalator, I was so distracted that I stumbled and fell. Lucky for me, some person had the sense to hit the emergency button to stop the moving stairs.

I proceeded on my trip and finished my work assignment in a fog. I found it challenging to stay focused on the needs of my clients. I was on autopilot, but mercifully my consulting skills kicked in, and my clients did not seem to notice anything wrong.

Several months later, when I returned from a business trip to England, Kris had constructed a memorial to Oaxaca on the Mexican holiday, the Day of the Dead. The shrine consisted of photos, flowers, cards, her food bowl, leash, collar, footprints made in clay hours before she died, and, of course, the orange rubber ball she had chased a thousand times. This ritual did not remove the grief. However, it was profoundly comforting to us. Grief is like a time-released capsule. But it never entirely goes away; it is just woven into the fabric of life.

We scattered her ashes on some of her favorite beaches on the Point Reyes seashore in Northern California. We console ourselves with the fact that we gave her a great life for her final seventeen months. We know it was far superior to her village wanderings in Oaxaca. We also thank her for opening us up to rescue dogs. I was not one to pick up a stray dog from the street or adopt a dog from a shelter. In fact, before Oaxaca, I was largely ignorant of the world of rescue dogs. All my past puppies had been from breeders or pet stores. Yet, today we have adopted two more—one from Costa Rica and one I found as an abandoned puppy in an old plastic shopping bag on the side of a road in Mexico.

My teacher, Oaxaca, made me realize I had put my love on hold for decades. She broke down the wall I had put up against loving freely. She also gave us the courage to adopt other dogs and give and receive unconditional love. From Oaxaca, I learned life is something you give away, but it also requires courage to absorb the loss. I thank Oaxaca for teaching me to open myself to hidden feelings of grief and love and to experience the Source through her more immediately. She created a safe space. She always seemed pleased to see me, even when I felt terrible. She also put me in touch with my history of abandonment.

In our society, with our bias toward happiness, we often stuff our feelings down when faced with suffering. Unfortunately, we also embrace the toxic positivity of "I'm fine" when nothing could be further from the truth. We resist viewing pain as a gift. I learned from loving Oaxaca with an open heart that when we resist or deny our sorrowful feelings, we miss an authentic connection with others in pain and a chance to expand our love beyond our comfort zone. Yes, that expansion of our interior self increases the intensity of grief, but it also reveals a certain beauty in suffering.

I had lost animals and people before and yet managed to choke off my feelings. Was it because my male conditioning told me big boys don't cry? Or was I fearful the sorrow would overwhelm me? Or was it that I had detached myself from painful feelings at an early age? Maybe it was all three.

I suspect now that love is more than a feeling. I don't have to cry to show my love. I can love through my actions, like when we adopted Oaxaca. And in return, she taught us having a dog is more than having a pet. Finally, *finally*, we had a loyal and faithful friend. And heaven knows we need friends in this broken and divided world. We can learn this from Confucianism, where friendship is a core relationship that undergirds society. Because of Oaxaca, I have no problem expressing my affection to the next two dogs we adopted. These dog teachers continue to humanize me.

Section Three

FAITH TODAY

Putting the Pieces Together

The advent of COVID-19, with its demand for social distancing, was a blessing in disguise. It brought me home, not to a physical space but to a resting place deep within. Over the next three years, I was snatched from my busyness and catapulted into a spiritual journey where I began to access the true nature of my being. Saint Augustine captures a similar interior movement in his *Confessions*: "You have made us for yourself, O Lord, and our hearts are restless until they rest in You." Whether we name this experience religiously as God, Soul, or psychologically as the True Self, the label does not really matter. Intuitively, we know our hunger is for something more profound. My moments of contact with the world of Spirit were few and far between. But when I did, mystery transcended understanding. In the words of St. Teresa of Avila quoted by Mirabai Starr, "I am like a drop of rain falling into a great ocean of the love of the Eternal One. First, I feel the splash, and then I'm absorbed in the vast expanse of salt water."

I recall several teaching moments during my movement away from the tribe. In retrospect, many of my current religious views would not have even been predicted in my tribal past. As a Baptist minister in the 1970s, I had zero knowledge about same-sex attraction and love and the thought that prayer was about listening and not talking. Moreover, the

Jesus of my beliefs was one-dimensional. He was the object of my studies but was not viewed as a social activist who bucked the religious and political establishment. Yet, he seldom engaged my heart.

As a preacher, I could carefully craft talking points about Jesus. But combing through the Scriptures did not necessarily make me a lover. Instead, it took numinous experiences to pluck the strings and of my heart, put me in touch with the stream of eternal consciousness, and create…

Chapter 13

I MET HER AT DAWN

I was leading a spiritual retreat for a group from my church. We were at a mountain getaway in Southern California in the 1970s. I had one foot in and one out of the tribe, and my spiritual director had introduced me to contemplative practices at the Jesuit Novitiate in Santa Barbara. In a sense, I was like the blind leading the blind as a neophyte in contemplation or meditation. There I was, a doctorate in psychology and white male confidence in hand, encouraging the whole group to go out alone into the woods for an hour of silence and listen for I did not know what.

The damp early morning mist enveloped me. The smell of pine infused my nasal passages and cleared my sinuses. A cup of freshly brewed steaming coffee warmed my hands and snapped my thoughts to attention. The process was like opening a book and waiting for some significant passage to jump at me. Instead, I lazily stared out over a mist-shrouded meadow as the sun began peering through the trees.

And there she was.

Less than twenty feet away, a young doe grazed silently in the meadow. She did not flinch when she sensed me. Instead, she raised her head and stared at me for an eternity.

In that meditative moment, she spoke to me. There was no audible voice, but a trace message formed in my mind from a Bible passage I learned as a child: "As the deer longs for the water, so I long for God" (Ps 42:1).

It caught my attention. I knew about that inchoate longing that originated from some inner self. Some would name it the Spirit of the Divine.

That early morning encounter generated wonder and devotion. So what happened that day to make my heart sing?

Chapter 14

LAUGHTER IN THE NIGHT

It came to me in the small hours of the night and disrupted my sleep. My usual strategy in such moments is to suspend any immediate judgment. I sat with the experience and let it percolate. Intuitively, I allowed the night terror to run its course. Something important happened here.

I came to the end of myself. Then, in desperation, I cried out to the I-do-not-know-what for help. Some would say I was praying. Was it a prelude to surrender? The accumulated rational answers of a lifetime did not work for me then.

"Are you there?" I asked.

The reply came in a flash, "Yes, I am."

I viewed myself on a split screen. Were these two parts of myself talking to each other? The one side seemed like some eternal part of the universe that had been there all along. It could have been beyond my skin as well. Yet, somehow, it was very familiar and had always been there.

I started laughing—a heaving belly laugh. Was this some secret cosmic joke? Why was laughter displacing my tears? Who was this cosmic jester? Yet it seemed genuine. Then, after a few minutes of mysterious joy, more tears flowed.

I heard singing. A woman was gently crooning a lullaby. Now, what was this? Was it an attempt to soothe me? Was it my mother's comforting voice? Was mother God singing in my soul? Then came more laughter. Was this a private joke between some revealed entity and me? Were these hallucinations? The experience was an extension of the split-screen-me from before.

My attempt at self-diagnosis faded. Instead, I yielded to a profound peace that rose from within. I was in the eye of the storm.

A door opened. A shaft of light filled the room. It was a full-on experience but very brief. After several moments it began to fade.

After the glow of the experience slowly faded, I wrote about it because I feared it was some middle-of-the-night illusion that would disappear. But, instead, because of my incredible sense of well-being, it became apparent grace had entered my life and touched me deeply. But, of course, I was skeptical about my interpretation of the event. So my first thought was, Will this last?

Chapter 15

A SOUL-BASED DREAM

I ran into an impenetrable rock cliff. I had been hacking through a dense jungle for several days, machete in hand. I was a man on a mission, hurrying to do something meaningful. I advanced toward my destination step by step, severing branch after branch. Finally, with tired limbs, sweaty brows, and a sore back, I was satisfied with my progress.

The forest opened into a meadow. Before me stood an imposing mountain of solid granite. *What now*, I thought. With no apparent options for forward movement, my frustration reached a boiling point. Somewhere from within I cried, "Move out of my way. I am the king of the world."

Silence.

"Don't you know who I am? I am the king of the world."

No response.

Then the mountain whispered, "You are not the king of the world."

Humbled and dumbfounded, I stood there for what seemed like an eternity. Eventually, I sputtered out, "You are right. I am not the king of the world."

A miracle appeared. The massive cliff face began to crumble. Boulders plummeted to the meadow where I stood. The rift in the mountain grew, and falling boulders smashed into smaller rocks and ground pebbles into gravel.

Through the dust, an image emerged. It was a young, vibrant sapling, standing green and tall amidst the chaos. It had been there all the time. It always would be there.

As I reflect on my dream, the declaration of my regal status represents the obstacle I encounter when I live from the ego (the thinking brain that is never satisfied, never at peace, and always attempting to be the controlling agent.)

The sapling speaks of my soul, the eternal spark in me that is my point of contact with the Divine. It's the God in me, my interior homing device.

Chapter 16

THE DAY I MET AN ANCESTOR

My wife's mother, Helen, had died the previous day. Apart from the grief of the loss, we were blown away by the daily "visits" she received from deceased friends, family, and forbears during her final days. Sometimes she reported the room was full of celestial visitors and commented to her caretakers, "Get me out of here; it's too busy."

Other times she talked and laughed with what we determined to be her mother, grandfather, and close friend.

With each image she experienced in her visions or visits, she seemed happy, even delighted, to see them. (Hospice staff routinely validate such experiences. These appearances are not viewed as delusional.)

The night after Helen's death, Kris sat at the window seat in our bedroom, looking out at the star-filled New Mexican sky. She was thinking of the already deceased, who may have come to help with her mother's transition. We had appealed to this cast of ancestors to please help Helen feel received in love. In one final message, Kris whispered to them, "If you're here and you can, or have the inclination, show me a sign."

The next afternoon we were sitting on our screened back porch where she had sent her mental telegram to heaven. In our conversation, Kris noticed a giant green bug on my elbow. Startled, she got up quickly and told me to stay very still. As she approached to brush off the strange bug, she exclaimed, "It's a praying mantis!"

She moved in closer to observe the mantis. It cocked its head to the side as if appraising her as well. At that moment, she decided to snap a photo with her phone, then gently brushed it off me. She said, "I've only seen one mantis here, and it was outside on the front porch several years ago."

As she finished her sentence, I noticed the praying mantis perched on Kris. "Now it's on your shoulder!" I exclaimed.

Carefully, we captured the mantis in a glass and took it outside, setting it free. We noticed that it chose to linger on the porch steps rather than leap away.

Kris reached for her computer to find out if the praying mantis had any symbolic significance. Years ago, she'd talked with a woman in our village about totem animals. The friend told her that a totem animal represents a spirit and that you don't choose your animal. Instead, the animal chooses you.

According to the South African National Biodiversity Institute, if you find a praying mantis inside your house, it indicates the presence of an ancestor. The Kalahari Bushmen in Africa worship and consider the praying mantis as the oldest symbol of God. They believed it to be an incarnation of God, and whenever they saw one, they would try and decipher its message.

Was this a sign or a coincidence? After all, Kris had asked for a response from the world beyond the veil. And how often does such an appearance materialize? More to the point, why can we not sense those who have passed on when they are closer than we think?

Recently we read how mythologist Joseph Campbell was once in his fourteenth-floor apartment in Manhattan, reading about how the praying mantis was a hero symbol in Bushman mythology. Campbell suddenly had a rare urge to go over to the window and open it. When he stuck his head out and peered to his right, he was startled to see a praying mantis staring at him.

A posting by Trish and Rob McGregor on the website *The Mystical Underground* captured my thinking about our and Campbell's experience: "Think about it. How many praying mantises hang out on the 14th-floor windowsills of Manhattan apartments?"

Kris had asked for a sign from the departed. Here's what she wrote:

"Was this it, in the form of a praying mantis? Or was it just a coincidence? On the porch, the mantis had landed first on you, and then, as if to make sure we got the message before we returned to our conversation and forgot, it also landed on me. As its human-like head and alien green eyes fixed firmly on my earthly brown ones, it seemed to be answering my question. Yes, we are here."

Describing the appearance of this magical creature as a coincidence takes the poetry out of the experience. It was one of those awe-inspiring, goose bumps revelations where the veil between this world and the next can sometimes seem very thin.

MY EXPANDING FAITH NOW EMBRACES THE STRONG POSsibility of dead folks appearing. In the past, my academic training taught me that everything I experience comes from within the walls of my brain. Any impressions, dreams, or visions come from many physical directions, including the collective unconscious. Likewise, my theological training taught me that the Big Kahuna in the sky damns anyone who consults a medium.

Does that mean that while death may end a person's life on earth, it's not necessarily the end of our relationship with them? Are my ancestors just a heartbeat away beyond the veil? Today I find myself communing with my mother, who, in her words, has gone home to her reward. I ask what she thinks about this or that in my life. I get the message, "Keep walking in the light!" Is this message luck, coincidence, or something rattling in my brain? I'm divided and at the experimental stage regarding meetings with departed ones. What the heck? Why not ask my mother what she thinks about this and that in my life? After all, if Roman Catholics can speak to their saints, why can't I speak with mine, my mother?

Internal experiences with the world of the Eternal One are a new frontier for my spiritual life. This internal shift in faith was from my head to my heart. But I was also exposed to external influences that produced seismic changes in my path to presence. For example, while intellectually I subscribed to the oneness of all, historically, I was a stranger to same-sex relationships. My education about the equality of all did not come from Bible study or the church but from personal relationships with LGBTQ+ friends. I also took a master class in oneness with some of my patients who happened to be gay. Another lesson came when I officiated at the wedding of two of my lesbian friends.

Chapter 17

WHEN LOVE CAME OUT OF THE CLOSET

As a straight male, I did not awaken to the presence of same-sex love until the mid-1980s, during the peak of the HIV/AIDS crisis in the US. The catastrophic disease surprised the nation, with few testing and treatment options available for most sexually-active gay males.

As a psychologist new to clinical practice, I had no knowledge or experience with same-sex love and HIV challenges. I was deeply steeped in the culture of evangelical Christianity, where ignorance and prejudice about people with different sexual orientations were rampant. During the epidemic, Baptist minister and faith healer Pat Robertson attempted to cure those infected by AIDS through prayer while declaring publicly that same-sex love was depraved and evil.

At that time, I was in my early forties and had recently moved to California from the Pacific Northwest. In Oregon, I was a professor of psychology at a Baptist Seminary. Although I was training others to become psychologists, I was still very much in the Baptist church fold—I was very familiar with prejudice against the LGBTQ community. In fact, I had been a Baptist minister myself in South Africa for five years.

During that tumultuous period, Jim (not his real name) came to see me as one of my first patients in California. He had heard about me at his evangelical church. At the time, I had my feet in two worlds. One was in a progressive Episcopal church with an active ministry to AIDS patients and their families. The church also had a couple of gay pastors on its staff. My other foot was still in the evangelical community, where I was identified as a "Christian" psychologist. Though I had never expressed my views on same-sex relationships, those who referred Christian patients to me assumed I was aligned with their dogmatic perspectives. Their referrals from evangelical churches quickly became most of my caseload.

At our first meeting, Jim seemed defensive. Despite the air-conditioning, he was visibly perspiring as he entered my office and scanned the room for my credentials. He stopped to stare at a dramatic Salvador Dali lithograph, "The Visceral Circle of the Cosmos," that adorned my wall. One of my patients described it as a person spilling their guts. That was the last thing Jim seemed to want to do that day.

Typically, my patients gravitated towards the comfortable seating and sank into the couch. In contrast, Jim chose a straight-backed chair and perched himself on the edge of the seat. From his body language, it was clear we would have to navigate trust issues.

Although a new therapist, I knew not to directly confront a patient's defenses. I sought to establish a safe space for my patients to explore sensitive or painful issues. I also knew that unconditional positive regard was a precondition for successful therapy.

Earlier that day, I had worked at a local psychiatric hospital. I'd had a busy day before Jim entered my office—I was fighting off weariness. Unlike other patients, Jim did not begin by telling me why he had come to see me, and I didn't ask. I started by taking his history. I asked about his family, and he said he was happily married with two young children. It was then that I asked, "Why did you come for therapy?"

He said, "I came to see you because you head up a Christian clinic. People from my church recommended you."

When I asked him why they recommended that he seek therapy, a dark cloud crossed Jim's face. He started to hedge and reiterated what was going well, especially with his family. He continued this defensive dance for several minutes. Then abruptly, he asked, "What's your position on gays? Are gays born that way, or do we have a choice?"

I thought to myself, *This is a test. He said, "We." Does that mean he's gay?*

I didn't know how to affirm his sexuality because I didn't understand his orientation—I was unschooled and ignorant. I avoided suggesting conversion therapy. I knew that the American Psychological Association had recently cautioned against it as there was insufficient evidence to support that psychotherapy changed a person's sexual orientation.

My past evangelical teaching had biased me to view same-sex attraction as "sinful," but of late, I had been questioning the biblical position that homosexuality was sinful. On the other hand, thinking of two males kissing or having sex made me cringe. Was that because it was wrong? Or was something amiss with me? I was confused.

Sitting across from Jim, I asked myself whether I should refer him to another therapist who was more skilled in dealing with gay men. Instead, I decided to hold off on the referral issue and dig deeper into Jim's story.

I asked him, "What's your theological position regarding a person's sexual orientation?" I already sensed the answer. Jim came from a church community that attempted to change people from their same-sex orientation through prayer. After a long pause, he must have decided it was safe to reveal his story.

With tear-filled eyes, he spoke softly, in almost a whisper. He said, "I'm gay, and I'm scared. I don't know what to do. Do I admit or suppress my feelings for men?" He paused, wiping away tears. The tears welled up again and he continued speaking. "What about my family? If I go with my feelings toward men, will I lose my family? On the other hand, I'm tired of putting on a mask to survive."

He looked at me helplessly and said, "My pastor goes on antigay rants from the pulpit. He makes me feel vile. He knows about my gay orientation. The only reason he doesn't approach me directly is because I'm married to a woman. So I can't talk to him anymore about being attracted to men. If I do, the church will prescribe that I go through their healing rituals. But I have a problem with that."

"What interventions are those?" I asked.

"Oh, everything from exorcisms to the so-called healing of the inner child. And intensive periods of prayer—you know, pray the gay away! My gay friends told me about this: a prayer group meets with you alone to pray."

"What do you think of this?" I said. "Do you think this would erase your attraction to men?"

"No! Gay friends in the church have secretly confessed to me that even after the church healing sessions, they never experienced the same sexual "whoosh" with females as they felt with men.

"I'm miserable. That's why I've come for therapy. I'm a Christian. I love my family. I don't want to lose my family or my church. Why won't the feelings just go away? Please, can you help me make those feelings go away?"

His appeal deeply troubled me. It was heartbreaking. He had revealed a fundamental truth about himself. As a straight male, I could love whomever I loved. Why didn't he have the right to love whomever he loved?

I wish I could have helped Jim, but I was still in the process of evolving. Patients like Jim helped me see the truth. I hope he is at peace and living his truth today.

Over the next several months, Jim's church referred a few more gay men for treatment, but it wasn't long before the pastor learned that I did not try to convert them. The referrals stopped. In later years, after I'd clarified the natural diversity of human sexuality and the right to love who you loved, I referred my gay patients to gay-friendly churches, often with openly gay clergy, who affirmed them for their sexual orientation.

As for Jim, he soon decided to terminate therapy. Jim was one of my first teachers on my path toward fully affirming same-sex love.

Recently, I was reminded of Jim when I read an opinion piece in the *New York Times*, "As a Gay Man I'll Never Be Normal" by Richard Morgan. Morgan wrote:

"Queerness was such a battle that all I wanted was peace. Every hill made me crave flatness. Every insult made me crave quiet. Every shove made me crave stillness. Every reminder of my different path made me yearn for a forgettable life."

About ten years later, after moving to Northern California, Kris and I were enjoying some time off work, walking the streets of San Francisco. As we approached Market Street, the roads were jammed with people celebrating. Suddenly we realized we had landed in the middle of a Gay Pride parade. With nowhere to move, we watched the parade pass by. It was my first gay pride parade. People were dressed in outrageous outfits, singing and dancing to music. Standing in my khaki pants and white button-down shirt, I was fascinated but very uncomfortable—I'd entered another world where I did not know how to behave. As men wearing dresses passed by, blowing their horns and calling out to the cheering crowd, I was drawn to a large group of mothers. They danced their way up the street with their arms around their adult male children, dancing in solidarity with them. I began to tear up. By then, I had a lot more experience—I had friends who were gay. I knew that when they "came out," they suffered rejection and hostility from their parents and friends, especially from my former tribe.

The week same-sex marriage (finally) became legal at the end of June 2013, I was standing in the hot sun with Kris at a wedding in a vineyard north of San Diego, wearing a new suit for the occasion. We were about to witness the wedding of our friends' lesbian daughter and her partner. I was not an audience member; I was the wedding officiant. After their vows, the excitement in the audience was palpable. Everyone was on their feet. The audience was already beginning to cheer and applaud for the final declaration. I turned to the audience and raised my voice above the cheers:

"I have been waiting for this day for years!"

In pride and gratitude, I made my declaration:

"By the authority vested in me by the State of California, I pronounce you wife and wife!"

Turning to them, I said, "You may now kiss each other." The audience roared and clapped in joy for the beautiful couple just married and also in acknowledgment of the wedding's historical significance.

I wish I had added, "And by the still higher authority of a loving Presence, I pronounce you wife and wife." Next time…

It was a big moment for California and banner day for a migrant from a church that would have summarily excommunicated me for officiating on such an occasion.

My personal growth culminated that day when I officiated in a legal same-sex marriage representing an expression of monogamous love and the right to love whomever you love.

That ceremony was a watershed moment in validating what was spiritually important to me—the equality of all persons, no matter their background or sexual orientation. There could be no compromise on my part. I viewed it as a validation of love and a human right. After I officiated at that wedding and posted a picture of the ceremony on my wife's social media, some tribe people unfriended her. I was hurt yet not surprised by such censure. It was a first for me because way back in South Africa, when I was a Baptist minister in the late 1960s, I knew nothing about homosexuality and gay marriage.

That wedding was an outward sign of my religious metamorphosis, yet, I still had a way to go toward an open heart. I needed to learn the wisdom and discipline of silence so that I could experience the world of Spirit holistically in the right hemisphere of my brain.

Chapter 18

SHUT UP AND PRAY

I'm praying but in a very different time and place. I am not talking now but listening for what I cannot anticipate or explain. It all started when a physician told me, "You have cancer."

The diagnosis should not have come as such a surprise. The medical tests showed rapidly rising PSA scores, and a biopsy revealed an aggressive form of prostate cancer. Although a cancer diagnosis is not necessarily a death sentence, mortality is one of the first things that come to mind. In blew a bunch of "What ifs?" What if the surgery is unsuccessful? What about the side effects of surgery, like impotence and incontinence? When I expressed my concern to the surgeon, with his dry gallows humor, he said, "Better wet than dead."

But, unfortunately, there was little comfort in his attempt at a joke. I was too preoccupied with the negative consequences of the surgery.

The prayer took place weeks after my diagnosis. I visited Wells Cathedral on a business trip to England in 2007. I find most cathedrals stifling and stuffy. However, the one in Wells is very feminine in its design. From the moment of one's entry, it wraps its arms around each person in a warm embrace. It is no coincidence that the cathedral is called the mother church of the diocese. Gothic in architectural style, Wells is one of the most beautiful and poetic English cathedrals that I've seen.

I usually visit a church when no one is present. The introvert in me loves solitude. As I sat silently in the vast space, I was confused. I reflected on the significance of the newly diagnosed cancer. Then, after several minutes on one of those uncomfortably hard church pews, out of the blue, I heard a soft voice: "When you pass through the waters, I'll be with you."

There it was! A voice! So who was there? Was it a passage from the Scriptures I learned as a child? Was it some universal Source? Or was I only talking to myself? Wherever that voice originated, it got my attention. A wave of comfort enveloped me. It echoed the English mystic, Julian of Norwich: "All will be well, and all will be well, and everything shall be well."

The lesson gleaned from the silence that day at Wells set the stage for future forays in listening for whatever. While the surgery diverted me from death's door, I still had life lessons to learn from a place of silence. My somewhat clumsy attempts at meditation each morning opened me up to periodic sources of strength and inspiration. But part of me still questions any voice or Presence I may feel in those quiet moments. However, acting as if these manifestations are objective is more helpful.

Prayer was not always about silence. In my early tribe days, it was about frenetic chatter directed at heaven. We informed God about the people that needed to be saved (converted), the wounds and illnesses that required healing (the organ recital), and, of course, there was always a confession of our sins and the request for forgiveness (the transgression dump). I once asked a priest what the Source would say about prayer. He quipped, "Shut up and listen."

When I embarked on this uncharted inner journey in silence, I was at a loss for where to find help. Then, on the recommendation of a friend, a former Jesuit novice, I sought spiritual direction. On my spiritual retreat, I asked my spiritual director and psychologist, Leo Rock, "What do I do in spiritual direction?"

Leo replied, "Nothing."

Such advice threw me for a loop. I come from a world of action. I live by notions of who is going to do what, and by when? My brain was constantly being pressed into action around problems to be solved. How could I measure progress without a project with measurable outcomes? The silence was uncomfortable and a threat. It gave my ego, the pest within, little room to move. Also, I could not control the unpredictability delivered by silence. Leo taught me not to wait for content to fill a vacant space. It is much like the discomfort we feel with pauses in a conversation. Instead of just sitting in silence, we often feel the compulsion to say something. Lessons from silence have been a part of my education in contemplation. I have learned that moments of stillness open me up to greater creativity (out-of-the-box thinking), mute my chattering mind, and grant access to the Divine spark within.

As a psychologist and executive coach, I value pauses in dialogue. I often use these occasions to ask for the inner Source of wisdom to instruct me by praying, "What's going on here?" or "Please give me the wisdom to see." More often than not, a comment emerges that shifts the direction of the conversation in a dramatically new direction. I love the ancient Hebrew priest Eli's advice to the boy Samuel: "Go and lie down, and if He calls you, say, 'Speak, Lord, for your servant is listening'" (1 Sam 3:9).

Silence in prayer is easier said than done. Any novice meditator like myself will testify that containing overactive thoughts is integral to any practice. Focusing on our breath can activate a thought muffler. We can sometimes disable the ego by instructing it: "You don't have a problem to solve." Taking it out of the game creates space for the true self to emerge.

Some years ago, I took a friend to our local meditation group in Mexico. He had never been to such a gathering before. After meditation, I asked him how he felt about the experience. He replied, "I prepared the outline for my university class for the next semester."

Before I am too quick to criticize my friend, let me admit that I have used meditation time to write an entire blog in my head. Talk about Restless Mind Syndrome! However, sometimes, in rare moments, my thoughts quiet and the line of sight to the other world becomes more apparent.

Another venue for generating awareness is often in nature. Many folks in the USA experience God in the natural world. I memorized a line from the Psalms long ago that speaks to the natural world's power: "Day to day pours forth speech, and night to night reveals knowledge" (Ps 19:2). As I immerse myself in the sounds of the river running through our property, the wind in the cottonwood trees, and the ravens calling each other in the early morning, at times I glimpse presence.

I often use the following exercise I learned from Fr. Richard Rohr. I repeat this sequence several times.

Be still and know that I am God.
Be still and know that I am.
Be still and know.
Be still.
Be.

In my prayer life I'm slowly starting to crave silence. It's in solitude that I open to the world of spirit and hear the gentle voice of love.

Chapter 19

A FOLLOWER OF JESUS

A lifetime ago, I was a leader in the tribe of evangelical Christianity. At that time, I knew quite a bit about the man from Nazareth. Theological studies filled my noggin. Degrees were tucked under my belt. But knowing "about" him did not mean I "knew" him.

Why's that? Well, there are two reasons. First, as I've explored in many places in this memoir, my heart was still closed to many of my emotions. Second, but more importantly, I was put off by the idea of Jesus which had been preached from the pulpits in the evangelical background I had grown up with. The sermon that to me is a prototype of judgmental religion is titled "Sinners in the Hands of an Angry God" by American preacher Jonathan Edwards in the 1700s. This emphasis on the wrath of God conjures up fiery scenes of hell. Today those same sinners on which the church heaps its vitriol are proponents of same-sex marriage, prophets that call society to task for endemic racism, and a servant spirit that opens the way for the disadvantaged to have a voice and receive equal justice and opportunity.

I read Jesus in the New Testament through a different lens. He would not be welcome in many tribal churches. He is also less a judge and more a compassionate lover who identifies with the marginalized. Yet, he is not some milquetoast, "anything goes" compromiser. As a revolutionary, he spoke truth to power, challenged the religious leaders of his day, and made enough good trouble to get him crucified by the Roman occupiers. He did not have an ounce of any establishment in him.

Similarly, Jesus, in his relationship with God, teaches us we are sons and daughters of the Eternal One. He was fully human. So are we. But he was more than his physical body, as we see in his appearances to his disciples after his death. He teaches us about the eternal nature of our consciousness. Whether we realize it or not, we have a part of that endless stream coursing in our souls.

In his daily practice, he personified presence. He was not just listening for the voice of God. The Divine voice came through him. We, too, can echo that divinity when we are aware of and embody our true selves. Through that nature and his empowering example, we can say of our oppressors who deeply hurt us, "Father, forgive them, for they know not what they do."

As the One who empowers me, Jesus shows me who I already am, the embodiment of the *imago Dei* (Image of God). From that place, I can let go of the hurts of my past and become the person I'm destined to be.

Jesus of Nazareth is not how he is often portrayed today. Tribal politics like Christian nationalism contaminate his person and mission. He is neither left nor right on the political spectrum. He is the lover of all and does not divide folks into saints and sinners, them and us, and Democrats or Republicans.

First of all, Jesus was not a Christian.

Also, his last name was not Christ.

Nor did he intend to start a religion named after himself.

That's the main theme of *The Universal Christ* by Richard Rohr: he sees Christ everywhere and not just in people. We, too, can be awakened to the Christ within. We are encouraged by the apostle Paul to "Let this mind be in you that was in Christ Jesus" (Phil 2:5). In this state of humility and surrender, we can live out our true or original selves, sparked by the Divine imprint.

When the early disciples met after his death, they told Jesus stories in typical Jewish fashion, through mythical and symbolic eyes. They did not view his life through the lens of literal interpretation. Instead, then as now, a symbolic understanding takes us into the Spirit of scriptural stories.

He was also not the blond-haired, blue-eyed, Ralph Lauren model type. Nor is he the white baby in the latest Mattel nativity scene. Instead, he was a dark-skinned Middle Easterner from the poorest of the poor communities, and he identified with those on the margins of life. Those working-class/peasant roots solicited contempt from the religious establishment. They mocked him with the meme, "Can anything good come from Nazareth?" (John 1:46).

Jesus was not an advocate for the wealthy ruling or religious class. He was not the prosperity gospel guy. Instead, Mary describes him as someone who "brought down the powerful from their thrones and lifted the lowly; he has filled the hungry with good things and sent the rich away empty" (Luke 1:52–53).

Over 2,000 verses in the Bible speak to our responsibility to the poor. So why do we cut funds for the homeless? What is the rationale for depriving minorities of their opportunity to vote? Why cancel mental health services, avoid building low-income housing, resist helping those about to be evicted from their homes, and punish refugees seeking asylum? And what justification is there to make Christianity a get-rich scheme?

The radical Jesus is not the president of some nanny state. Nor is he a bleeding-heart liberal. Instead, he is clear-eyed, compassionate, and reflects the mercy of God.

I have studied the life of Jesus for decades, taught classes on his words and deeds, published books on the topic, been an ordained evangelical minister, and was a devout (as measured by conformity) Christian for most of my early years.

Today, I am inclined to list myself as a follower of this radical first-century teacher. Some divine force is arm-wrestling me to walk in his shoes. This way, he teaches me authentic spirituality is the antithesis of the cult of the self. It is not about getting, attaining, achieving, performing, or succeeding—all of which tend to pander to the ego. Instead, it is more about letting go of what we don't need. It is more about humility and less about puffed-up pride.

He was the One who said, "The son of man has no place to rest his head" (Luke 9:58b). Simplicity and detachment marked his life. He was drawn more toward anonymity and did not crave celebrity status.

I recently read Andrew Boyd's article called "Monotheism at Thirty Thousand Feet." By listing my religion as "none," I realized I was throwing the baby out with the bathwater. I needed to revisit that radical and mystical figure and experience his love in new ways. I resonate with Andrew Boyd, who writes, "I could approach the Bible stories to use (Karen) Armstrong's words as 'symbols of a more elusive truth.' I could try to understand Jesus not as the literal son of God but as a healer and preacher who stressed his weak, mortal humanity. Looking through the lens of comparative religion, I could see Jesus as a Jewish bodhisattva—a spiritually gifted hero willing to put off his enlightenment for the sake of others. And through the lens of Latin American liberation theology, I could make a common cause with him as a revolutionary champion of the oppressed, urging us to care for the poor and ask why the poor are poor.

As embodied divinity, Jesus is a mirror or imprint of presence. He models a selfless dedication to his disciples then and now. He teaches us we don't need authority to tell us what to think or know. Instead, the Master shows us how we can draw on the resources of our interior life to be what we already are. His message is, "Follow my example by becoming the love you already are." He demonstrates our hope in knowing the Eternal One is already there. The Eternal Spirit moves us into a life of service and love. All we need to do is surrender to this inner divinity. After all, he told us, "The kingdom of God is within you" (Luke 17:21).

This recounting of my journey is not a "been there, done that" list. I'm still a neophyte and will be on the brink of discovery for the rest of my life. *Hearts Wide Open* is also largely aspirational. I'm not there yet. I still feel my heart constricted in its capacity to love. However, I'm certainly not treading water on this faith journey.

My true self continues to be teased out by whatever life throws at me. I feel those levels of consciousness hovering in the wings. I cry more than I did in the past. My silent prayer life is a catalyst that loosens the hard soil in my unconscious mind where past hurts lurk and constrict my heart. Prayer is the cleansing agent that scrubs my unconscious mind of part burdens.

That's the gift that comes from writing a memoir. It is also the gift of grace.

Chapter 20

A JOURNEY INTO GRACE

Surrounded by this natural sanctuary, I experience the world beyond my five senses. Some mysterious consciousness leaves my cluttered mind behind.

I'm released from my former religious life's constrictions and devastating disappointments in this breakaway moment.

I'm no longer held hostage to past beliefs.

Nobody asks, "What do you think about God?" and then rejects me because I experience Divinity differently. I'm not required to shapeshift into an orthodox impression of Christianity and to the cultural or ecclesiastical prescriptions that once tied me up in knots.

Here, Source meets me on its own terms.

We are taking an early morning hike on Trader's Trail just south of Taos, New Mexico. It's a 2-mile shot across a vast, sage-covered plateau towards the Rio Grande River gorge. No one is there. The brisk morning air jolts me out of my repetitive thoughts. The earth's fragrance is strong from the previous night's rain.

To the North, the snow-capped Sangre De Cristo Mountains take me to an internal refrain.

"I will lift up my eyes unto the hills from whence comes my help? My help comes from…"

Far off to the South, I see the flat-topped mountain of Perdernal, where artist Georgia O' Keefe found her inspiration. Her ashes are scattered on its peak. She wrote:

"When I stand alone with the earth and the sky, a feeling of something in me going off in every direction into the unknown of infinity means more to me than anything any organized religion gives me."

Tears stream down my cheeks, and I stop on the trail. Overwhelmed by gratitude, I find myself starting to sing an old hymn…

> Loved with everlasting love,
> drawn by grace that love to know,
> Spirit sent from Presence above,
> thou dost witness it is so.
> O this full and precious peace
> from the Presence of all divine
> in a love that cannot cease,
> I am God's, and God is mine.

One thing I know for sure is I am eternally loved. The roots penetrate deep into the nurturing love of my mother and scattered remnants of Scripture like "nothing can separate me from the love of God." Waves of grace buoyed my soul. Something far more significant than anything I've concocted for my life emerges from the Divine in me.

I'm now at one with the surrounding beauty.

The veil between this life and the next is paper-thin. My ancestors are no longer dead folks; much like the Native American religion and the Day of the Dead celebration, the spirits of departed friends and family swirl around me. They are right here and smile blessings on me. I thank my mother and others for all their gifts, including protection and guidance. They are there. I don't hear voices, but I feel how I felt when they were alive.

With a heightened sense of presence, I catch another glimpse of grace through the heart's portal. My feet are on the doorstep of some mysterious home. That day, I experienced overwhelming joy and remembered one of my favorite quotes from Adyashanti in "Falling Into Grace."

In those moments when we know we don't know when we take the backward step, heart wide open, we fall into grace.

References

Adyashanti. *Falling into Grace: Insights on the End of Suffering.* Boulder, Colorado: Sounds True, 2011, 231.

Saint Augustine. *Confessions.* Oxford: Oxford World's Classics, 2009.

Baldwin, James. "As Much Truth as One Can Bear." *The New York Times Book Review.* January 14, 1962.

Bourgeault, Cynthia. *Centering Prayer and Inner Awakening.* Boulder, Colorado: Cowley Publications, 2004, 162–164.

Boyd, Andrew, "Monotheism at Thirty Thousand Feet." *Sun Magazine*, May 2020.

Brueggemann, Walter. *Tenacious Solidarity: Biblical Provocations on Race, Religion, Climate, and the Economy.* Philadelphia: Fortress Press, 2018, 384.

Johnson, Cedric B. *Christian Conversion: Biblical and Psychological Perspectives: Lee Edward Travis interview,* Doctoral dissertation. Fuller Graduate School of Psychology, Pasadena, 1978.

Johnson, Cedric B. *The Psychology of Biblical Interpretation.* Grand Rapids: Zondervan, 1984.

Julian of Norwich. *All Will Be Well.* Notre Dame: Ave Maria Press, 2008.

McGregor, Trish, and Rob McGregor. "Joseph Campbell and the Praying Mantis." The Mystical Underground Website, 2009.

Moore, Thomas. *A Religion of One's Own: A Guide to Creating a Personal Spirituality in a Secular World*. New York: Avery, 2015, 56.

Morgan, Richard, "As a Gay Man, I'll Never be Normal." *The New York Times Opinion*. June 26, 2023.

Rohr, Richard. *The Universal Christ: How a Forgotten Reality Can Change Everything We See, Hope for, and Believe*. New York: Convergent Books, 2021.

Spong, John Shelby *Biblical Literalism: A Gentile Heresy*. San Francisco: Harper One, 2016.

Starr, Mirabai. *The Interior Castle by Teresa of Avila*. New York Riverhead Books, 2003.

Steinem, Gloria. *The Truth Will Set You Free but First it Will Piss You Off*. New York: Random House, 2019.

Stevenson, Bryan. *Just Mercy: A Story of Justice and Redemption*. New York: Spiegel and Grau, 2014, 17.

Walsch, Neale Donald. Facebook post. July 22, 2014.

Wilkerson, Isabel. *Caste: The Origins of Our Discontents*. New York: Random House, 2020, 103.

Wolfson, Laura Esther. "The Holiness Hidden Within the World, Rabbi Rachel Timoner on Rediscovering Judaism" *Sun Magazine*, October 2018.

Acknowledgments

A village came together for this memoir barn raising. To say it's "my" book would be an exaggeration. Too many others came alongside and gave significant input, talked me off the ledge when I felt stuck, and gave honest feedback when I needed it the most.

Without Kris, my wife of more than twenty-five years, this book would not have happened. She put up with me when I was a million miles away in my head, gave me tough writing advice, and helped rewrite some of the more challenging portions of the manuscript. Our regular morning talks over coffee have stimulated many ideas in this memoir. Our lives intersect at so many points. You can see that throughout this book. Thank you, thank you, Kris.

Then there is Julie Mars, writing teacher, coach, and editor extraordinaire, who wrestled sense and meaning into my manuscript. She kept me honest about the challenge of writing and taught me to slow down and be patient. Recently, Julie told me she had been reviewing dozens of the documents I had sent for her review. On every front page I had written "Final Draft." I had a long way to go in learning about the craft of writing! Without Julie, my book would have been dead in the water.

I acknowledge the contribution of two churches in my spiritual pilgrimage. All Saints Episcopal Church in Beverly Hills, during the tenure of Rector Carol Anderson, nurtured me in the contemplative tradition of Christianity and grounded me in my faith when my world seemed to be falling apart. All Saints Episcopal Church in Pasadena, under the leadership of Rector George Regas, shaped my sense of oneness with all and introduced me to Jesus the revolutionary. The words that welcome all to the Eucharist, "Whoever you are and wherever you find yourself on this faith journey, you are welcome at our table," are engraved in my heart and are embedded in my sense of the inclusiveness of my faith.

Made in the USA
Middletown, DE
30 May 2024

55068773R00076